COMPUTER SECURITY
Businesses at Risk

R.R.C. PENFOLD

ROBERT HALE · LONDON

Robert Hale Limited
Clerkenwell House
Clerkenwell Green
London EC1R 0HT

2 4 6 8 10 9 7 5 3 1

Typeset by
Derek Doyle and Associates, Mold.
Printed in Great Britain by
St Edmundsbury Press Limited, Bury St Edmunds
and bound by
WBC Book Manufacturers Limited, Bridgend

Contents

Author's Note

Throughout this book the term 'hacker' is used to describe the people who break into computer systems, which is slightly unfair to the hacking community. In fact a hacker is someone who delves deep into systems so as to understand them better, both for their own benefit and for that of others. (Many software companies like to hold back a few details of their products to give themselves an added advantage. For example, if it is difficult to convert from one file format to another, users might decide to stick with the supplier they have rather than buy a similar product off a rival who uses that different format. By finding out how the conversion can be done, hackers level the playing field between small start-up companies and giant multinationals, which forces them to compete on price and service – the way it should be.)

The people who break into systems are actually called crackers, although as the media has so blurred the distinction between the two in the minds of most people they mean the same thing. For this reason the term hacker has been used here simply to prevent confusion (although one should bear in mind that there is a difference, and that difference is important). At the very least a knowledge of the right terminology will help to make what the media calls cyberspace a more comprehensible place in which to do business. Better yet, it makes it a place where business is actually possible.

1 Why Computer Security is Important

There is no such thing as a good reason for someone to lose their job, but one of the worst reasons of all must be because the company went into liquidation as the result of a catastrophic data loss. It just adds insult to injury that this could have been prevented by the application of a few simple rules!

Perhaps this sounds unduly alarmist. But is it? In 1993 a report commissioned by IBM discovered that less than 25 per cent of all companies had a viable contingency plan for coping with computer failure. It also discovered that a full 70 per cent of the companies that experienced a computer failure ceased operating within eighteen months. That may seem an incredibly high figure – until one considers the consequences of data loss:

Cash flow is reduced. Without information stored on the computer, invoices cannot be created. Without invoices, no one will pay their bills.

Deliveries cannot be made. No one knows what has to be delivered where. True, the order book can be recreated from paper-based records, but not immediately – and for companies operating in rapid-turnover, fast-delivery markets that delay could prove fatal.

9

Credibility is lost. That same failure to meet orders makes customers less likely to trust the company in future, leading to an erosion of the customer base.

Financial penalties could be invoked. Delays caused by computer failure could lead to deadlines being missed. If penalty clauses are involved, this can have disastrous financial consequences.

Orders cannot be accepted. If no one knows what items are in stock, how can orders for them be taken? The company faces the impossible choice between accepting an order in the hope stock is available, then failing to meet it and losing a customer, or just turning the order down and losing the business that way.

Production could be lost. Without adequate stock-control information there will be a delay in ordering raw materials. This could result in their late delivery, and production lines standing idle. The more companies adopt just-in-time techniques, the more critical this will become.

Any company that suffered such a data loss would very likely find itself paying the interest on a very large bank loan, taken out to pay its suppliers and employees, while its customers were migrating elsewhere. In these circumstances the real surprise is not that so many companies fail, but that some actually survive.

Anybody who is still unconvinced should consider the results of the *Information Security Breaches Survey 1998*, sponsored by the National Computer Centre (NCC), the Department for Trade and Industry, ICL Computers and ITSEC (UK IT Security Evaluation and Certification). This is a bi-annual survey carried out across all industry sectors and all sizes of company within each individual sector. As such it is a highly authoritative document which must, therefore, be taken seriously. This makes it all the more frightening as of all the companies contacted no fewer than 44 per cent reported a significant security breach in the previous two years. It is also worth reporting that of all the companies who suffered a security breach, large or small, a massive 53 per cent admitted the problem could have been prevented. (In other words it was entirely their fault.)

To make matters worse when the NCC followed up these cases they discovered that the actual costs were, in fact, underreported. While the cost of reinstating the service was considered companies failed to take account of other factors such as the cost of replacing lost data. When these were also considered the total costs were on average three times the reported costs. Because of this the NCC has calculated that the total cost to all businesses due to security breaches could run into billions of pounds – and that just in the last two years – although they are understandably reluctant to state an exact figure.

As a measure of how much money is being lost consider the following results taken from the security survey, but remember these show reported losses. The true cost is likely to be up to three times higher.

Average cost of security breach

By number of employees		By breach type	
1–9	£2,949	Theft of equipment	£17,557
10–99	£1,165	Viruses	£3,690
100–499	£5,359	Power failure	£2,920
500+	£20,199	LAN failure	£446
		User error	£416

In the light of such figures, anyone still not worried by the problem of computer security should seriously consider reducing their daily intake of tranquilizers.

Alternatively they might care to consider the Data Protection Principles as laid down in the 1984 Data Protection Act. In this case the eighth principle is relevant as it states:

> Appropriate security measures shall be taken against unauthorised access to, or alteration, disclosure or destruction of, personal data and against accidental loss or destruction of personal data.

As the act covers payroll and personnel information then any management who failed to take adequate precautions against breaches in computer security would not only have to cope with a massive financial loss, they could also face criminal prosecution.

Computer security – or, to be more precise, the protection of computer systems and the data stored in them – is therefore an important subject. Without trying to oversell the issue, it is, in a very real sense, something on which the entire survival of the organization could depend. The traditional head-in-the-sand, it-won't-happen-here attitude is no longer good enough. Computers, like every other device, are subject to failure and theft. Fraud and virus attacks are always a possibility. And from time to time even the most benevolent organization will upset its employees and risk having them fill the system with bogus information. (When this actually happened to one company it cost an immediate £50,000 to put right, with an estimated long-term cost of £2.5 million.)

The point is, it *could* happen here. And, in a world where even something as simple as a spilt cup of coffee could knock a computer out of action, the problem will never go away. That is why anyone who is, or aspires to be, in senior management should look closely at their own security arrangements with a sharply critical eye.

*

Fortunately the solution is relatively straightforward. It requires no special expertise, nor is it expensive. In most cases security can be improved without incurring any cost whatsoever – which makes it all the stranger that companies are prepared to allow such risks to develop. Unless a company has a corporate death wish, it should make the procedures involved mandatory and enshrine them in its disciplinary code.

To begin with the problem should be broken down into its two separate components: keeping the computer system safe from physical damage and making the data secure against theft or fraud. Each is equally important, but each needs to be tackled in a different way. In fact most companies come to grief by failing to recognize that there are two sides to the issue: those with highly sophisticated security systems forget to protect themselves against computer failure and those with all manner of backup devices forget about security. Unfortunately, though, unless both aspects are adequately covered, the system has to be considered as being at risk and highly vulnerable.

Remember that, in this particular context, security does not mean military secrets of interest only to special agents with 00 prefixes. In industry a vast amount of information is commercially sensitive; its disclosure could harm the organization or benefit a rival, which comes to the same thing. Examples include:

Market research.
New product launch plans.
Proposed quotations for contracts open to tender.
Product cost details.
Research not yet covered by patent.
Information affecting the share price of a company or its clients.
Information covered by the Data Protection Act.

13

*

These are just a few examples. With no effort at all anyone could find literally dozens more, simply by looking around their own organization and asking two questions:

How much would it cost, or harm, the company if that data became disclosed or damaged?
How much would it benefit a competitor to have access to that data?

The company that asks itself those questions has already done more to protect itself than most others. Implicitly, it has also taken things one stage further and decided that, if these problems do occur, it is best that they happen to a rival. In a highly competitive world, commercial advantage rests with the companies whose data is secure. They are the ones who can cherry-pick the best orders from the company that has suddenly been blighted by computer failure.

It pays, therefore, to have a system that is as safe as possible. No system can be entirely secure, but almost all can be improved by a study of the categories into which all security breaches fall. These are:

Hardware-related:	Software-related:
Computer failure	Viruses
Power failure	Fraud
Fire	Data theft
Flood	Error
Lightning	Misuse
Sabotage	
Theft	

With the exception of computer networks, which pose their own security problems in addition to those mentioned above, all systems can be protected by the application of a few basic princi-ples specific to the particular area of threat. These principles are simple and straightforward and not difficult to learn or to imple-ment. They begin with the contingency plan.

2 The Contingency Plan

Obviously no-one can predict the fire or flood that completely destroys the computer building, still less a terrorist bomb. Yet on Saturday 24 April 1993 a bomb in the Bishopsgate area of London totally destroyed the offices of the Banco de Sicilia – and on the following Monday the bank was open for business. Rapid recovery is possible, even from the worst of disasters. All it takes is careful planning.

In the high-stress environment of an organization suddenly deprived of its computer, trying to produce some quick fix on the day itself will be close to impossible. Extra equipment or staff may be needed, new ways of working may have to be decided and new methods of reporting created – none of this can be implemented instantaneously. The thinking must be done *before* the event. The plan must be ready in advance, if only to serve as an emotional support at a time when, as Kipling says, 'all about you are losing their heads and blaming it on you'.

It goes without saying that keeping all data regularly backed up is vital (so vital that it rates a chapter all by itself). Surprisingly perhaps, backup strategies have no place in the contingency plan – but this is because backing up data is *so* important, *so* fundamental, that it should be done *regardless* of any other security requirements. If an organization ignores everything else but backing up data, it will at least still exist; if it fails to do this, the information it depends on is lost, and every other security precaution will be no more than an exercise in futility.

Everything else must be considered, though, which means that real work has to be done, and real time spent doing it. This has got to be understood from the beginning. Preparing a contingency plan will never be, and can never be, a five-minute job. Too much is at stake. So, daunting as it sounds, take the trouble, take the time, and remember that the whole process revolves around a single key question:

When the computer fails, what will it take to keep the business running?

If need be outside consultants can be brought in – but only to give advice, not to draw up the plan itself. To be truly effective the plan should be prepared by someone who thoroughly understands the organization. Better yet, there should be someone in the organization who thoroughly understands the plan.

Fortunately guidelines do exist. Of necessity, these are rather general, nevertheless they can be used to produce a viable contingency plan that will be ready to protect the organization when the worst happens.

They begin with the most obvious:

The General Approach

Start at the Top

This applies to any aspect of security, but it is particularly relevant to computer security. Without management support at the very highest level the scheme will either be ignored because of the work involved, or else be implemented half-heartedly and then allowed to fall into disuse. Needless to say, either alternative is potentially fatal – and yet perfectly natural. No one will be happy about taking on extra work that cannot be quantified and does not directly contribute to departmental objectives. This is why top management support is so vital. (It is also worth mentioning that directors have a legally binding 'duty of care' towards the assets at their disposal. Now that information is increasingly being considered as a corporate asset, this is in itself reason enough to take a close interest in the contingency plan.)

The Chief Executive must either take personal charge of the project, or else appoint a named individual to do so. At the same time, the Chief Executive must make it clear that anyone hoping to have a career within the organization ignores the project at their peril. Without such a clear, unambiguous statement nothing will happen, and the organization will remain forever vulnerable.

Ignore the Arguments

This follows on naturally. Even with a clear statement of intent from the top, hard-pressed managers are still likely to argue the point. The best counter to such arguments is to look at the same problem from a different point of view. If any part of the system is so busy, so overworked, that it cannot spare the time for anything else, then that in itself proves just how important disaster recovery procedures are – both to the organization as a whole and to the department which, in order to do its job, apparently relies on the system operating at maximum capacity.

Moreover, anyone asked to make recommendations must be made to respond by a set date. This not only helps to create a sense of urgency which is needed considering that disaster could strike at any moment, but would also force managers to do the job and not leave it forever in the pending tray. In the modern organization each sub-system relies on the others; the output from one is an input to another. In practice this means there can be no such thing as a partial solution. Should just one part of the system be left uncovered then the organization that relies on that system has no protection.

There always will be arguments, they have to be expected, but they must be overcome. Disaster recovery is too important to be ignored.

Analyse the Problem

Before a contingency plan can even begin to be prepared, there must be a clear understanding of the risks being faced. Here 'risks' means not just the different possible causes of disaster (although these must obviously be taken into consideration) but also the effects of that disaster. In this way individual components of the overall system can be divided into those that are critical to the business – and so need to be restored immediately – and those that can wait. In other words, concentrate on the important like invoicing and order taking and leave the rest to later.

It is also important to consider how long it might take before the computer system becomes available again. As with so much of contingency planning this is impossible to quantify for every company in every industry and for every problem, but there are at least average figures available. According to the *Information Security Breaches Survey 1996*, the time to recover from an incident was at least one week in the following percentage of cases, by category:

Fire	32%
Theft	30%
Flood	15%
Computer failure	15%
Wide-area network failure	14%
Local-area network failure	7.5%
Viruses	7.5%

20

The survey also notes that:

> In 56% of the security incidents which involved an interruption to
> normal processing it took over one day to restore the affected
> systems to complete operation.

Obviously there are problems in relying on averages, but, if nothing else, these figures do show the potential scale of the disasters
which contingency planning is intended to avoid.

To recap: Know what equipment is vital to the business and
know how long the business might have to do without it. From
that knowledge, a sound plan can be drawn up, and any costs
involved can easily be justified – or, to be more exact, the costs of
contingency planning can be justified once the cost of *not* having
a contingency plan are known.

This leads us on to the question of how much it will cost the
company to be without its computer. Here the costs involved can
be broken down under three headings.

Recoverability of data. If the data can be recovered – from
paper-based records for example – then there is no cost.
However, if data cannot be recovered – for example, telephone sales orders, which exist only in the computer – then
the cost must be the average value of such orders for the
time when the computer is off-line.

Personnel downtime. If some people are entirely dependent
on the computer to do their job then they still have to be
paid. The amount they get paid for doing no work is therefore part of the cost of computer downtime. If they then
have to work overtime to re-enter that data from other
sources, e.g. paper-based records, this too is a cost that must
be taken into consideration.

Lost image. If the company cannot work as normal it will give
a poor, or non-existent, service to its customers, which will

reflect badly on the organization as a whole. That, in turn, will cause the company to be seen as unreliable, and this could result in a fall in new orders. To calculate this cost, either use the experience of the sales staff, who know how stable their customer base is, or else fall back on a rough-and-ready calculation. According to those who have studied the problem, the cost of lost image works out at 0.1 per cent of annual turnover for each day of computer downtime.

Ignore the Experts

Strange as it may seem, the only people who should never be asked to produce an organization-wide contingency plan are members of the IT Department, the computer professionals. The reason for this boils down to objectives and priorities. The IT Department is there to look after the computer; that is *its* objective, but not necessarily that of the organization as a whole. When the system goes down the first priority is to get the *business* going again – the computer can wait.

Only the Stock-control Manager can decide how to maintain stock control without computer support. In the same way, only the Sales Manager knows how to keep the sales function going. Like all the other departmental heads, only they can know what will work, and they should be free to decide that without interference. Obviously a degree of co-ordination is required, and information needed by one department from another has got to be included in the supplier department's emergency procedures; however, none of this needs the technical help of a computer department.

There is only one area where the IT Department should be consulted. Assuming the computer system has been well designed, it should include something known as graceful degradation. Simply stated, this means that, if disaster strikes, the entire system will not immediately collapse, but parts of it will remain operational. Exactly which parts obviously depends on the nature of the disaster (it is even possible that different problems will cause different elements of the system to fail). The point is that only the IT Department can know about this, which is why they should be consulted – if only so a range of options can be prepared. Different plans for different disasters is a very sensible arrangement.

The foregoing might be described as an overview of contingency planning, containing as yet very little of the nuts and bolts of the operation. Nevertheless it is worth pausing for a moment to assimilate the broad picture, because too often the general principles can become hidden under detail.

The key point is that someone must take charge of the contingency plan. One named individual – with the authority of senior management – must be ready to act as co-ordinator, sergeant-major and, if the need arises, even instructor. It is this person who will have to settle conflicting demands for scarce resources, make sure all the departmental plans mesh together and authorize any necessary expenditure.

This individual can then allocate work on the plan among others. Spreading the workload amongst various groups or departments helps create a sense of involvement. It also means that when disaster strikes everyone knows what to do without reference to the co-ordinator, who might not even be there on the day.

The Specifics

The general rules are simple, therefore. However, there is more to it than that. The plan itself still has to be produced. Once again, however, guidelines are available. Some will concern only the people actually doing the job; others may involve the co-ordinator.

23

In all cases, though, they will provide a framework around which a viable plan can be built. As before, they begin with the obvious:

Set priorities

Consider only what is essential to keep the business running. Everything else can be classed as a luxury until the system is running normally again. If nothing else, this will at least cut down the workload for the contingency planners.

Re-Use Staff

Almost every department will have some members of staff doing jobs, like data entry, which begin and end with the computer. It therefore follows that when the computer is down these people can be reallocated. Alternatively, staff in other departments could be free, in which case they could be borrowed – assuming this has been agreed beforehand.

Maintain Paper-Based Records

Many companies, trying to move towards the paperless office, store all their day-to-day information on a computer and only produce management-control reports once a month. This might be perfectly acceptable in ordinary circumstances, but it does mean that the organization will be deprived of all its valuable data if the computer goes down mid-month. For some companies this will not be much of a problem, but those involved in fast-moving industries will be stopped dead in their tracks.

This makes it obvious just how valuable it would be to have a print-out showing stock details, despatches, requests for quotation, or whatever else the organization relies on. Depending entirely on the nature of the industry these print-outs could be produced every day, every other day, or even once a week. The sole criterion is that the information they contain will still be accurate enough to be useful.

One other point has to be remembered. If printing out this information is the first job of the day, then, if the disaster happens during the night, the organization will be denied the data just when it needs it most. To guard against this, make the print-out the last job of the day before. That way the organization either has the data immediately to hand, or else, if the problem occurs in the evening, it has until the following morning to solve its problem.

Expect Only Competence

Virtually every office has its own unofficial computer guru, a man (and it is usually a man) considered to be the local expert. Such people are always offering advice, even when no one is asking for it, and the temptation is strong to make use of them during an emergency. This should at all times be avoided.

The problem with these people is that their level of expertise can be difficult to judge. They may indeed be highly knowledge-able – or they may be the proverbial one-eyed man in the king-dom of the blind. No one can know for sure which they are until they are put to the test – and the height of an emergency is the wrong time to discover the poseurs.

All any manager can rightfully expect from their staff is competence. To ask for more not only courts disaster, it also makes the entire plan dependent on the right people being there at the right time. If they are absent or leave the organization, then the plan falls apart.

Some people might certainly be asked to do a job outside their normal routine – like a data-entry clerk keeping a manual record of orders – but all that takes is competence; no extra skill is required. That is as it should be. As long as no one is asked to do more than meet the basic demands of the job, no one will cause any unwelcome surprises.

Make Sure Staff is Available

This follows on from the previous points. When the plans are drawn up they are highly likely to show that extra staff will be needed in the event of a disaster. If so confirm their availability in advance. Just because the organization already has an account with a secretarial or temp agency, it does not necessarily follow that these people will be immediately available. The agency may insist on a certain period of notice, and anyone responsible for contingency planning must know about that – and be prepared to look elsewhere if need be.

When catastrophe strikes everyone will be under pressure. Having the telephone number of an agency which claims to be able to deliver the right people immediately might, in reality, do very little to relieve that pressure, but it will save time and a lot of fruitless phone calls.

Obsolete Equipment can still be Useful

When a new computer system is installed, the old one can still be a valuable backup device. By definition it was once capable of running the company system, and in an emergency it could do the same again, always assuming certain precautions are taken. According to conventional wisdom, any reserve equipment should be kept in a separate building from the one that houses the main computer; in this way the fire or flood which destroys the main system leaves the secondary unit untouched. That is fine up to a point, but, if cost prohibits this, a different part of the same building could be adequate (just). Put the main and reserve computers as far apart as possible, so that at least one of them should survive a partial fire or flood, and leave it at that. Instead concentrate on everything else that needs to be thought of.

Software licences will need to be checked. Running two systems could mean double the amount of software. It could

26

also mean running different versions, because on new PCs new software is introduced to make use of the much more powerful machines now being produced. (If this is not the case, backup copies of the software could be made quite legally and installed on the reserve equipment only when needed.)

The reserve system will only be created slowly. This applies only to systems run on a PC network. The reserve system will only be built up as old computers become available after being replaced by new ones. In this case, identify the essential core elements of the system and implement those first; the rest can be added later.

Handbooks might be needed. If software is to be used at a separate location, then extra copies of handbooks, manuals or other documentation might also be needed. If the computer room is inaccessible for any reason, then so, too, would be the handbooks. Having extra copies would therefore be a good idea, but always consider the security implications: it might be necessary to keep them under lock and key.

The network is unnecessary. Computers are connected together over a network to make working easier, not to make it feasible in the first place. For a short-term emergency measure, files that would once have been transmitted across the network could be copied to floppy disk and passed around the office.

So, a reserve system could be created simply by not discarding obsolete equipment. However, as with everything else in life, once the spare capacity exists other uses will be found for it. Obvious examples are training or system development, both of which could help to make the project cost-effective. However, always remember the main purpose of having a reserve system. The emergency facilities it offers will be next to useless if they cannot be immediately accessed. Even if training and systems development is seen as an important part of the reserve system's function, its *raison d'être* is disaster recovery.

If Extra Equipment is Needed, Have it Available

A secondary backup system is not a feasible solution if computers are leased, or just not ready for replacement. In such cases, if the organization cannot survive without computer support, then alternatives have to be found. Fairly obviously this means either hiring PCs or renting time on another mainframe, and agencies do exist to provide these services.

As with extra staff, if extra PCs are to be hired, the question must be asked: can they be delivered immediately? Software is not a problem for PCs – if it can run on one it can run on any other, but in the world of the mainframe nothing is that straightforward. Mainframes run on proprietary systems, so it would be a very wise move to check that an agency computer can accept the organization's data.

For organizations handling vast amounts of data it would also be a good idea to make sure the agency has the capacity to process it within a reasonable time. The best way to do this, of course, is to try it out using the backup data files: the exact information the computer is expected to handle. That way an assurance can become a guarantee.

There are disaster-recovery specialists who can provide a Portakabin-style office, complete with computers and office equipment, at almost the proverbial moment's notice. In times of crisis this could be a life-saver, but (again) check first. Confirm the price, confirm the delivery time and, most of all, confirm that all the equipment is suitable. If so, the telephone number of the company concerned should be included in the contingency plan.

In much the same way, some companies can offer a full office suite for a disaster-struck company to move into. Before taking that option, however, check the location of these offices. For companies operating in a major city centre they may be local and convenient, but this will not necessarily be true for businesses out of town.

Consider Redundancy

In most aspects of business the term 'redundancy' is emotive in the extreme. In information-technology terms, though, it simply means having excess capacity to hand. For example, networks could adopt a process known as server mirroring, using two file-servers instead of the usual one. These might share the processing load between them, or one might stand idle, but, so long as either can handle the full load, then if one fails the other takes over immediately with no loss to the business. Although this is an expensive option, for companies where the computer is critical any expense could be recouped at the very first incident.

Consider Data Recovery

Specialist companies exist who can recover data from damaged disks or tapes. This might be a cheaper, or faster, option than trying to re-create lost data; in some cases it might be the only option available. In any case data-recovery specialists should be found before the disaster, not after. The questions to ask are:

What is their success rate, specifically with your type of equipment and operating system?
Do they have a 'clean room', where disk drives can be opened under dust-free conditions?
If the drive is opened, how will that affect hardware warranties?

Will the work be done in-house or subcontracted?
How quickly will data be returned?
Can they work on backup tapes?
Can the data be kept confidential?
Do they have engineers available to work on site?
Could they work round the clock?

From time to time all companies will have data on a floppy disk that is unreadable. The value of the data might be marginal, but sending the disk to the data-recovery company would still offer a golden opportunity to check their efficiency and reliability.

From all this it should by now be obvious that preparing a contingency plan is nowhere near as difficult as it probably looked at the outset. Nor is it expensive. In fact all it really costs is time (though it has to be admitted that in most companies time is the scarcest resource of all). Preparing such a plan is well worth doing, and the only sensible way of looking at it is to see it in the same light as an insurance policy: under normal circumstances it is just an extra expense, but when things go wrong it is a life-saver.

Working Up

However, the job of preparing the plan is still not over. Once all the departmental or group leaders have given their assessments, once they have been drawn together into a co-ordinated whole, and once extra equipment or personnel are known to be available at a moment's notice, there still, unfortunately, remains more work to be done. Like the new product which works well on paper, a lot more is needed before it becomes a saleable, or workable, item.

Once again the good news is that guidelines exist to help with the next part of the process.

Designate Contacts with the Outside World

If the computer goes down, a lot of people outside the organization have to be told: suppliers, customers, sometimes even the press. Designated individuals should be appointed to do this. That way, not only will the job be done, just as importantly, it will only be done once. (Customers might appreciate being kept informed of any problems, but if too many people all ring up to tell them the same thing the phrase 'headless chicken' will spring to mind.)

Like the phone numbers for the equipment-hire companies or the staff agencies, a list of names and addresses of people to be informed if the computer system fails could be included in the company security policy document. Alternatively, it could be kept separately. Either way, anyone charged with making contact should have a minimum of two copies: one for the office and one to be kept at home. If access to the building is denied because of some catastrophe, the phone numbers will still be needed – and will still be available.

Paper Exercises can be Useful

Sometimes called 'walk-throughs', these exercises involve all those involved in disaster planning sitting around a conference table (or an office) discussing what actions would be taken in the event of any problem the collected team can devise. This should then be continuously expanded to see if the problem really can be solved and, if so, how. As an added refinement, technical staff from the major hardware or software suppliers should also be invited; their in-depth product knowledge could be invaluable.

Accept Nothing Until it has been Proved

A saying frequently heard is that a contingency plan is just a collection of good ideas. Usually this means that what works in theory does not always work in practice. Therefore, no matter how sensible, realistic or logical any proposal sounds, accept nothing unless it can be proved to work. Too often some unexpected factor can appear which turns all previous calculations upside down and which, always remember, could have a domino effect on every other aspect of the plan. An example here would be something like asking a secretary to take down telephone sales orders and then finding she did it using shorthand which no one else in the Sales Department could understand. For reasons like this every single element of the contingency plan should be tried in advance to confirm they will work as expected. The choice is between finding out before the plan has been finalized – or finding out only after disaster has struck.

Review Constantly

Like the Production Plan, the Sales Plan or any other business plan, the contingency plan refers to a specific situation at a specific time. What works for one level of business volume may be totally inadequate for another; or a new product could add an extra degree of complexity. Unless the plan is constantly reviewed against current circumstances no one will ever know if it is likely to work.

At the very least, a time should be set when the plan should next be reviewed. However, it should not be ignored until then; any change to the business volume, the product mix or (needless to say) the computer system should trigger a review automatically.

Rehearse all Procedures

Fire drills are carried out on a regular basis for the excellent reason that when the worst happens everyone needs to know what to do. In much the same way, when the computer goes

down everyone needs to be well practised in the recovery procedure; a plan on paper is no substitute for a well-rehearsed, well-
drilled staff. The advantage gained from practice, in terms of
reaction time and expertise, far outweighs the disruption – and
anyway only full-blooded rehearsals can show up any pitfalls
and test the ways to avoid them.

And Afterwards

Not every system failure will be a total, full blown disaster; some
will create only minor inconveniences affecting a small part of the
organization, and their effects will sometimes be over before the
day is out. Nonetheless, whether the crisis is large or small, it
should all be looked at in the same light: as a way of testing both
the computer system itself and the disaster-recovery procedures.
If this is done, then flaws in the former can be rectified and refine-
ments added to the latter. This highlights the next rule of contingency planning:

When the emergency is over conduct a full post mortem.

Lightning *can* strike in the same place twice, and surviving the
first strike gives absolutely no grounds for complacency.
   Another good idea is to keep a disaster-recovery log detailing
what happened, why it happened and what was done to put it
right. In this way the experience gained in solving one problem
can be reused to solve others, with the additional advantage that
a permanent record can be used to spot trends or recurring
events. It can even be used as a basis for improving the system –
and that, by itself, is enough to justify the effort.
   The next point applies to stock-holding organizations only.
During the crisis, when monitoring procedures are at full stretch,
it is beyond belief that all goods movements will be recorded

precisely, or that they will be subsequently entered into the computer without loss of accuracy. Normal human error, compounded by the sort of 'can do, let the paperwork wait' mentality which usually appears on these occasions, will effectively make the stock file the least reliable document in the building. To expect otherwise is to ask the impossible. From this comes the next rule:

When the computer is back on line hold a full stock count.

Find the errors before they become problems.

As every organization is unique in some way, the best a set of generalized guidelines can do is to point managers in the right direction. If anything, the main value of such guidelines lies in showing how simple contingency planning can be, and how little expertise it calls for. Most of the rules fall under the heading of common sense and very few of them involve any extra expenditure. Nowadays it is even possible to buy software which guides inexperienced managers through every step of the contingency-planning process, even including assigning time scales to the various tasks involved. Anyone who can handle project-management software can handle contingency-planning software.

In other words anyone can do it. All that is needed is to answer the questions and address the issues raised in this chapter. Beyond that, only one point has to be remembered:

A computer failure is not an information technology problem. It is a business problem!

3   Data Backup

It is not the least exaggeration to say that the biggest single improvement that can be made to corporate information security is the regular backing up of data. Without this, even the smallest computer failure becomes cataclysmic. Yet the number of companies which run such a risk is truly frightening. According to one survey, only 8 per cent of PCs are attached to backup devices. This leaves a massive 92 per cent waiting for the axe to fall: far too high a figure for anyone to be comfortable with.

The Information Security Breaches Survey 1996 notes that:

> the most common failure involved loss of data due to a malfunction of the backup system or backup media or a failure to carry out backups according to procedure.

Backing up data is not vital – it is infinitely more important than that.

It has to be done, of that there can be no question. The next steps, therefore, are to consider what types of backup device are available, which files should be backed up and how backing up should be done.

Devices

The alternatives are:

Floppy disk
Hard disk
Tape
Magneto-optical disk
Redundant Array of Inexpensive Disks (RAID)

The Floppy Disk

This is the easiest and cheapest method of all. The data is simply copied from the hard drive to a floppy. No extra equipment is needed, and the disks are freely available. In fact, for anyone who has only a limited amount of data to be backed up it is pointless looking any further.

The BACKUP command included in the operating system (DOS/Windows) will do this automatically; the RESTORE command transfers data in the opposite direction, from floppy disk back to hard drive. However, about the one thing all the experts seem to agree on is that these commands should never be used. The problem is they can be specific to a particular version of the DOS operating system, so that data backed up from one computer will not necessarily load straight into another machine running on a different version. (To put that another way, if the original machine is damaged or stolen, it might not be possible to restore the data from backup disks to its replacement, which would very likely have a later version of DOS.)

The answer is to use the COPY command, either through DOS or through File Manager/Windows Explorer in Windows. This is just as easy, and it works between all versions of the DOS operating system.

The Hard Disk

Backing up data to a different part of the same hard disk can have its uses. If a file is lost or accidentally deleted a reserve file is immediately available – always assuming the disk itself can be accessed. If a fault occurs that prevents access to that disk, then both data and backup copy will be lost. To guard against this a second hard drive would be an obvious solution – although the temptation to use it for extra data storage, rather than for backup, usually becomes overwhelming. In addition, any hard disk permanently attached to a PC is open to virus infection. Of course, if the computer itself is stolen the hard disks it contains also disappear, however many may be fitted.

Fortunately there is such a thing as a removable hard disk. As the name suggests, this is a hard disk that can be physically removed from the machine for safe storage. This overcomes the problems of fixed hard disks being fixed and yet retains their tried and tested technology. However, nothing in life is simple, and decisions still have to be taken between the different types of removable hard disk drive on the market.

Broadly speaking, these fall into two distinct categories, best described as external and internal. External drives (also known as parallel-port devices) are sealed units, containing both disk and drive mechanism, which plug into the computer through its parallel port, hence their name. Because of the rate at which data can pass through this port, their rate of data transfer is slow, but their chief drawback is that they are sealed units, so there is no room to expand the amount of storage space available on the drive.

Internal devices, on the other hand, have their drive mechanism permanently attached to the computer. This mechanism accepts removable cartridges, which fit into a specially designed cradle in exactly the same way as a floppy disk fits into its drive unit. The difference is that with removable cartridges there are separate technologies to choose from. Some manufacturers ally the standard Winchester technology, found in all hard drives, to cartridges that are more rugged, to withstand the extra handling they will be given. Bernoulli drives use a different technology. They take their name from Daniel Bernoulli, an eighteenth-century Swiss physicist who explained how objects react on the surface of fast-moving fluids. In this case the fluid is air, and the Bernoulli effect pulls the disk towards the read/write heads, but the same aerodynamics keep the read/write heads from actually touching the disk. This makes the drive almost immune to head crashes (damage caused to the disk when rough handling causes the read/write heads to smash into it).

Taken altogether then, removable hard drives can offer a viable backup system. Fast, efficient and easy to use, they have a lot to offer, but only at a price. Cartridges and the cradles to hold them are not cheap.

Magnetic Tape

Despite advances in other areas magnetic tape is still the most cost-effective method of backing up data. It has its disadvantages (all data is stored sequentially, which can make the retrieval of a particular file a time-consuming process), but it remains superior in terms of cost and overall reliability. Very likely this has something to do with the fact that manufacturers have, between them, agreed on a set of standards which makes their products compatible with each other, and therefore interchangeable. After that, market forces alone keeps tape streamers highly competitive.

The first, and most important, of these standards can be traced back to November 1987 when the Quarter Inch Committee was formed. Although initially intended as a forum for technical matters, this almost inevitably developed into a standard-setting body, and so the QIC standards came into being. Originally these specified tape size (for example QIC-40 and QIC-80 referred to tape sizes of 40mb and 80mb respectively), but since then further standards have been added. Now everything from the basic drive interface to the magnetic heads have been specified. This can make for a confusing array of numbers, but nonetheless the fact that standards exist can only be good news for the end user.

However, QIC is not the only standard on the market. There is also Digital Audio Tape (DAT). This, according to its suppliers, has a number of advantages, the most relevant being the ability to store more data. To do this, data is laid down in strips tilted at six degrees from the axis of the tape, very much like the method used in video recorders. Unfortunately, QIC technology lays down its data horizontally, so the two are incompatible. It is therefore very much a case of reviewing the options and making a decision, based on individual needs, between the QIC standard and the DAT standard, which is known as Digital Data Storage (DDS).

Either way, magnetic tape can be fragile, so the following procedure is good advice, no matter what the standard used.

Do not leave a tape in the drive.
Keep the tape in its container when not in use.
Do not touch the tape surface.
Keep the heads clean.
Avoid exposure to direct sunlight, high temperatures or moisture.
Store tapes in an upright position, to prevent uneven winding.
If tapes are stored away from their normal operating environment they should be allowed to acclimatize for at least twenty-four hours before use.

Finally, if you choose a tape storage medium be careful about the storage capacity quoted by the manufacturer. This will usually be the amount of data that can be stored on a cartridge at maximum compression, which does not necessarily reflect normal usage in the real world.

Magneto-Optical Disks

This is the hi-tech, high cost end of the market. Few standards exist, and even the terminology seems designed to confuse. For example, Write Once Read Many (WORM) drives fall into this category, even though their main use is in archiving rather than backup. Under this system, data – for example, a legal document – can be stored on the disk, but can never be altered. If revisions are made, they are stored elsewhere on the disk. In this way the software will always display the latest version, but an audit trail exists detailing what changes were made and when. Since they are as secure as a hand-written ledger, WORM drives are naturally popular with the legal and accounting professions.

True Magneto-Optical (MO) disks can be written to many times, and it is important to be aware of this difference. These are disks coated with a magnetic material which can only be changed at high temperatures. A laser is therefore used to provide the heat, while an electromagnet changes the polarity in much the same way as a normal read/write head writes data to a normal disk. The difference is that MO disks cannot be corrupted by electromagnetic interference, or a disgruntled employee with a magnet, and data stored on them has a longer shelf life. Most suppliers will quote an average of fifty years for MO disks, whereas magnetic tape can deteriorate after only three.

For organizations where document retrieval is an important part of the business process, MO disks or WORM drives can be invaluable. Like everything else in life, though, they come at a price.

Redundant Array of Inexpensive Disks

This technology is for networks only. Basically, instead of one disk storing everything, several disks are used. They may be used in a variety of configurations. Sometimes data is stored across all disks, sometimes it is stored on one disk and duplicated on another, but in all cases the underlying principle is the same: if data is stored on more than one disk, then a single disk failure leaves the organization unharmed. Systems like this come into their own in places where data cannot be re-created using conventional backup techniques – for example, mail-order companies where customer orders and details are entered straight into the computer during a telephone call.

In principle this sounds easy, but in practice five levels of RAID technology have been defined. (There are actually several more, but these are either implemented by a specific manufacturer or have yet to be ratified by the standards committee.)

RAID-O. All RAID levels use a technique called data striping, which involves spreading data across all the disks. RAID-O uses sector striping. (All disks are divided into sectors, and data is written to them one sector at a time. Usually this would be on the same disk, but with RAID technology each sector is on a different disk.) All disks are read simultaneously, so the time taken to access a particular file is much reduced, but as the failure of a single disk makes the data unreadable RAID-O should not be considered secure.

RAID-1. This involves disk mirroring or duplexing. Disks are divided into pairs, and data written to one is automatically copied to the other; if the first disk fails, the second can take over. Multiple failures can even be coped with, always provided the failures are not mirrored to each other.

RAID-2. As well as disk mirroring, this also involves a much more sophisticated system of data striping which incorporates error-detection and -correction techniques similar to those found in communications packages, ensuring that the data is accurately duplicated.

RAID-3. RAID-2 is more appropriate for mainframes, while RAID-3 is a slightly less well-engineered version for PCs.

RAID-4. Check codes used to confirm the validity of the data are stored on a separate disk within the array. If one disk becomes corrupted, these check codes, plus the remaining disks, can be used to reconstruct the data.

RAID-5. Check codes are spread evenly across all the disks so there is no single point of failure.

Although it is not strictly a backup system, nevertheless RAID technology can offer increased protection against data loss, and as such it should be given careful consideration *in combination with other backup systems*. RAID technology cannot prevent the fire, flood or theft that would leave the organization helpless.

Which Files Should Be Backed Up?

The next point to consider is which files should be backed up. It is all too easy to look after the actual data and forget that other files can be equally important when it comes to restoring a computer system back to its original settings. These include:

All programme installation disks.
All .INI and .GRP files from the Windows directories.
CONFIG.SYS and AUTOEXEC.BAT files from the root directory.
All SET, SETUP and CONFIG files from the applications directories.
Setup information used by memory managers, hard disk managers or data caches.
Script files for connecting to networks, online services or other systems.
The RESTORE part of the backup software.

The programme installation disks should be copied, so that if a computer is damaged or stolen the applications it ran can be

42

installed on a replacement. At the same time, remember to make a complete backup copy of any software that has been upgraded or modified in any way. The manufacturer might have released a new version of a particular piece of software, or just a small piece of code to solve a particular problem (known as a patch or a bug fix), and this must be backed up as soon as it is installed. If not, restoring that application to a new computer would mean installing the original programme followed by all the upgrades and patches in exactly the right chronological order (because these will frequently overwrite the same piece of code within the program). Getting that right would be difficult enough in perfect circumstances; doing it while under pressure to get a system up and running again verges on the impossible.

All the other files mentioned above hold setup information which customizes each machine to an individual user's preference. Over time this can mature and change and should be backed up regularly. As for the RESTORE part of the backup software, if the computer holding this program becomes unavailable for any reason, it will be impossible to make use of the backed up data. To avoid this, and to save a lot of embarrassment, make sure a duplicate copy of RESTORE exists.

How To Do Backups

Of course all of this assumes that backing up can be done easily, at a touch of the proverbial button. There is in fact a lot more to it than that, but fortunately the rules are simple and should be followed for that reason alone. The primary one is to give data backup the same level of priority as banking the day's cheques. Both represent the life-blood of the company, so both should be treated equally.

Usually it is best if one person in authority is given the job as part of their normal working day, with another competent person deputized to cover for absences. Leaving backup to the individual user is almost a guarantee that it will be ignored, probably due to pressure of work. For the same reason it is best to schedule the process for lunchtime, when computer use, and network traffic, is nil. That way the demands of backup will not conflict with the inevitable last-minute rush job. After that all it takes is to do the actual backup itself.

For this, specialist software is available, sometimes bundled with the backup device, and in most cases this is easy to use once the terminology is understood. Software developers have the frequently irritating habit of assuming everyone understands the terms and forget to provide a plain-English translation regardless of their target market. In this case, however, the terms used, which are also the options offered by the software, can be easily explained:

Restore. The process of returning files from the backup medium to the computer they were taken from originally – or, in the event of a disaster, to another computer.

Verification. The process of selectively restoring certain files to make sure that backup has been successfully achieved.

Full Backup. Every single file is backed up.

Incremental Backup. Only those files created or changed since the last backup are copied.

Differential Backup. Only those files created or changed since the last *full* backup are copied.

Partial Backup. A term referring to either incremental or differential backups, to distinguish them from full backups.

As to why there should be so many different types of backup, that too can be easily explained. While a full backup is obviously the safest and best, it can also be very time-consuming, which is where the various forms of partial backup come into their own.

With an incremental backup the job can be done very quickly, so that (for example) a full backup could be made on a Friday, with only the changes being recorded on Monday to Thursday. This carries with it the advantage of recording the complete history of each file – what changes were made when – not to mention the fact that if a file is deleted one day and needed the next it can be recovered from the backup. Where this method loses out is in the time it takes to restore: the last full backup has to be restored first, followed by each incremental backup in turn. This can take a very long time, especially if the entire organization is held up waiting for it to be finished.

This is where differential backups score. Using this method the last full backup is restored, followed by the differential backup – much quicker to do. But if the organization creates or changes large amounts of data, differential backups can soon take as long to do as full backups.

Once again there is no clear-cut answer other than to match the method to the demands of the organization.

Next, always remember that, whatever method is chosen, the job has to be done regularly. Usually the best way of doing this is to establish a routine that becomes part of the working day: just another job to do rather than an additional chore. As a minimum:

Schedule the task for a specific time each day – and stick to it.

Appoint one person and give them full responsibility.

Do not rely on one copy of important data. Run the backup procedure a second time, however, rather than copying the first backup, because an error in the first copy would be transferred to the second.

A minimum of month-end and year-end backups should be stored off site. Use a specialist firm if data is sensitive.

Include verification as part of the backup process.

Retire old tapes and ensure tapes stored for long periods are regularly retensioned.

Occasionally try restoring a few files from an archived tape, to make sure neither head wear nor misalignment has made them unreadable.

If there is such a thing as a golden rule for backups it has to be never rely on the backup medium. Always do regular backups on to different disks or tapes, using them in rotation, so that if one fails the precious information can still be retrieved. Over the years a number of different strategies have been designed to do exactly this of which the two most widely used are:

Round Robin or Father-Son Principle

Do a full backup on a Friday, followed by incremental backups to the same tapes (or disks) every working day until the following Friday. Then do a full backup to a different tape and start the process all over again. Do this for as many tapes as there are in the set, at which point start with the first tape all over again.

Although in theory there could be just two tapes in the set, in practice three should be the absolute minimum with four or five recommended. That way if one disk or tape becomes worn out or unable to hold its data other copies will still exist. And if companies need to store more than four or five weeks worth of data all they have to do is increase the number of tapes being used.

Tower of Hanoi, or Grandfather-Father-Son Principle

Start as for the Round Robin above, but at the end of each month do a full backup to a new tape as well as to the tape in the existing set. Repeat this procedure for the next two months, after which time reuse the first tapes holding the monthly back-ups.

This procedure has been carried over to PCs from the world of mainframes where it has been shown to provide protection against virtually all forms of data loss.

*

No matter which method is chosen always remember the number of tapes in the set are for a single backup only. Anyone who wants to make a second backup, which is recommended, will obviously need a second set of tapes. Even without that a lot of tapes will be used so, again at the risk of stating the obvious, label every single one of them. Something simple like 'Friday 3' or 'Wednesday 1' would do, just so long as everyone knows what that means and which files that particular tape holds. A simple handwritten note is all it takes; alternatively the software could provide a printout of the contents of each tape although the tape itself would still have to be labelled so everyone knows what list refers to what tape. For organizations with a lot of data, or where the computers have a complicated directory structure to be remembered, the latter could be the easiest solution. It is even possible for the list to be stored on computer, but, if this is done, that file must be backed up too.

Where computers are concerned there is no such thing as being overprotective. If they can go wrong, they will – and even if they work, the backup could fail, which is the next thing to be checked. Every once in a while, just to be sure, restore the data from the tape or disk. Not only will it prove that data can actually be recovered from the backup medium, but the practice gained will be invaluable when disaster strikes. At the same time it might be worth considering the tape or disk itself. Like any magnetic material it can wear out and should be replaced regularly. The recommended frequency of this is thirteen weeks although a lot depends on usage. The time scale can be adjusted, but, even so, always err on the side of caution. No matter what the price of the tape, the data stored on it is still worth more.

Finally give some thought to where these backups will be stored. Keeping them alongside the computer might seem like a good idea, but that means that the fire or flood that destroys the computer will also destroy the backups. The best place of all is in a different building at least twenty miles away so that if the very worst happens and the emergency services have a large area cordoned off, due to the accidental release of toxic chemicals for example, which prevents employees reaching their own building the data will still be available. A bank safety deposit box is also a good idea, but if they must be stored on site a fireproof safe is the only sensible option available. Even so, a note of caution must be sounded. The chemicals built into these safes vaporize when hot, in order to keep the contents cool, so at least forty-eight hours must elapse before the safe can be opened. (Any less than that and the pressure build-up from the vaporized chemicals could seriously injure anyone opening the safe.) This is a point that should be noted not only for safety but also for its implications for any organization where the contingency plan calls for those backup tapes to be immediately available.

The whole message of data backup is to keep it safe, keep it secure and keep as many copies of it as you can. Then, no matter what other problems arise, the information that the entire organization depends on will always be available.

4 Power Supply Problems

The problem with computers is that they run on electricity. More than that, they need it to within very tight specifications: too much power can damage delicate computer circuitry, while if there is too little, or none at all, then any data not saved will be lost. In other words, yet more problems for the concerned manager to worry about!

That might not seem important, but these power surges can do a tremendous amount of damage even if the cause is just other electrical equipment on the same circuit. When the power of a lightning strike is added to the equation the problem becomes serious indeed and not just due to the chances of a building being hit by lightning. During an electrical storm powerful forces are at work which can have catastrophic implications for data processing equipment.

Protection Against Power Surges

When lightning strikes it always takes the easiest route to earth, often by going through telephone or power lines. This is one of the ways in which it causes power surges. The second comes from the intense pulse of electromagnetic radiation that it produces.

When this passes through a wire a current is induced in that wire which is more than high enough to damage a computer or printer. These two effects together create a serious problem. Nevertheless, there is a whole range of simple and cost-free precautions that can go a long way towards making the system safer.

Keep Cables Away From Lightning Conductors

Any cables running close to the down lead from a lightning conductor will be prone to high-voltage pulses. So, when lightning strikes, the building may be safe, but if the computer inside it is connected to such a cable, it will be at risk.

Keep Cables Away From Mains Power Lines

Power surges in the mains power lines can induce corresponding surges in network or printer cables if these run alongside them for any significant distance.

Unplug Computers When Not in Use

The switches on the sides of computers are often too lightweight to cope with power surges. On occasion electricity can jump across the air gap in the switch and cause damage. All this can be easily prevented simply by pulling out the plug.

Always Leave Modems Plugged In

Being more or less permanently attached to phone lines, which are themselves susceptible to lightning strike, modems usually have built in circuit protection (this should be checked with the manufacturer). As this works by leaking the current to earth, removing the mains plug would have the effect of disengaging the safety measures.

Keep Cables Short

The longer the lead, the greater the danger of a current being induced in it. Keeping cables as short as possible is such a simple precaution that it seems pointless to run extra risks by not taking it.

Use Shielded Cable

Ribbon cable might be cheap, and it might even be fitted as standard, but it offers no protection. Replacing it with shielded cable will repay the investment many times over during an electrical storm.

Consider Fitting Suppressors

Small mains suppressors are available and provide a cheap method of power protection – although, it has to be said, companies which specialize in mains protection will often describe the level of protection they provide as illusory.

Higher-specification surge and spike arrestors come in two types, providing coarse and fine protection. Coarse protectors handle high levels of energy, but are comparatively slow-acting, while fine protectors are faster, but can only handle low levels of energy. As these two types need to be used in combination they can often be bought as a single unit. If they are bought separately, coarse protectors could be used where the power enters the building and fine protectors placed on each computer. Beyond that the process becomes complicated enough to make employing a specialist worthwhile.

Keep Networks on the Same Circuit

When data is passed across a network as a series of electrical signals, there also has to be another wire carrying zero voltage, so that the electrical signal can be compared with a known zero constant. The computer works on the voltage difference between the signal wire and the null or zero wire. As this is so fundamental to the operation of a network, another connection is made with the equipment's earth wire to establish a common reference voltage known as a ground loop. Under normal circumstances this should remain at zero volts, but any power surge fed to earth by any equipment on the circuit interferes with that and creates power where there should be none. This effect (known as inter-system ground noise) prevents the network operating efficiently, causing garbled messages at best or crashed systems and damaged hardware at worst. It becomes increasingly common as more equipment is connected to the circuit (each item is a potential source of power surges), so the best advice is to keep all units of the network connected to the same circuit. That way any power problems will at least affect the system evenly, which is a lot safer than risking an imbalance between different ground loops. For complete safety, of course, the network should be on its own, separate, circuit.

Uninterruptible Power Supplies

The telephone and power companies have installed equipment to minimize the potential damage from power surges reaching customers through their supply lines, but even so, this can never be totally effective. For example, if the utility company's protection equipment is in a substation several miles away, then lightning striking the line between that substation and the office or home will completely bypass the safety precautions. Despite everything, the system will be vulnerable.

Ironically, the measures taken to provide protection are also the cause of further problems for the computer user. When high-voltage spikes are detected, automatic circuitry cuts in to isolate the supply from that line. Then, after about ten seconds, the same circuitry reconnects the line, and normal service is resumed.

Unfortunately, that ten seconds of power loss is more than enough to wipe out any data – assuming the microchip has not already been fried.

Fortunately, help is at hand in the shape of a device known as an Uninterruptible Power Supply (UPS). Despite its name, this is not a power supply, nor can it prevent power cuts. What it can do is to provide an emergency reserve of power, so that, in the event of a power failure, computer systems can be shut down without loss. As an added bonus, it can also safeguard the system against damaging power surges.

In essence a UPS is just a battery that switches in automatically whenever the mains supply fails, giving at least enough power to save any data and close the system down gradually. However, a modern UPS can do much more than that. Technology is now built into these devices which can cure all manner of problems, ranging from total power failure to those annoying glitches which beset any computer, and they now offer protection even to companies who had no idea they needed it.

To explain that, and to show how these problems can arise, it might be best if some of the terms used were first explained:

Blackout: Unsurprisingly, this means a total loss of power.

Brownout: A short-term decrease in voltage levels which can result in the loss or corruption of data. Brownouts are most usually caused by the start-up power demands of electrical devices like machine tools, motors or lifts.

EMI: Electromagnetic Interference, which is, naturally, generated by any electromagnetic device, such as a generator, industrial equipment or even fluorescent lighting. This causes those glitches and can introduce errors either in application programs or data.

Impulse: A sudden dramatic increase in voltage caused by such things as lightning strikes. Unprotected systems can suffer extreme damage due to this.

Noise: The name for either electromagnetic interference, radio-frequency interference, or both of these combined.

RFI: Radio-frequency interference, caused by such things as radio transmitters or mobile phones. Its effects are the same as for EMI.

Spike: Another name for an impulse.

Surge: A short-term increase in voltage which can stress electronic components. This is usually caused by switching off high-powered electrical devices, such as air-conditioners.

In some cases the software provided with the UPS can monitor power faults, which can be extremely useful to anyone so afflicted. Knowing exactly when brownouts or surges occur can help to identify the cause of the problem by matching this to other events in the building.

As an aside, it might also be worth looking at exactly where computers are positioned with regard to other equipment. In a shop-floor environment this is particularly true, especially if part of the manufacturing process involves spark erosion or radio-frequency welding. Even in an office, though, a lot of irritation (or worse) can be saved just by something as simple as keeping computers away from the photocopier. Failing that, consider the advantages of an uninterruptible power supply.

For those who want to give their arguments a solid foundation, a simple cost analysis has been designed to quantify the benefits of a UPS, and indeed to help to determine whether one should be fitted at all. It starts with the premise that even a slight power failure will cause a user to either restart (reboot) their computer or, alternatively, to log back on to the network. In either case this results in a loss of productivity which can be measured by multiplying the time taken by the number of times it happens in a year. After that a costing can be produced just by incorporating an employee's hourly wage rate into the calculation – remembering, of course, that it must include every employee affected.

To show how that works in practice, consider the following example:

A) Time for each user to log on/re-boot — 5 mins
B) Number of users — 9
C) Number of power failures per year — 30

Time lost through power failures each year (A × B × C)	1,350 mins
	(22½ hours)
Average hourly wage rate	£5.60
Cost of power failure each year (22.5 × £5.60)	£126.00
Cost of power failures over three years	£378.00
Cost of power failures over five years	£630.00

As the price of these units starts at less than £100 all of a sudden buying a UPS seems to be a good investment – especially as this calculation does not include such things as the cost of lost data, equipment damage or consultancy fees.

Needless to say, this being the computer industry, there is no such thing as one standard device. As ever, competing technologies are at work, so there are in fact three different types of UPS – offline, line-interactive and online – and each suits a different set of circumstances and requirements. Understanding what those differences are is the first step in deciding which UPS is right for a particular organization.

Offline

This is the simplest, most basic, form. It is connected between mains supply and the computer, and electricity passes through the device the way a TV signal passes through a video recorder on its way to a television set. Like a video recorder, all the UPS does is to clean up the signal by removing any noise or surges. When the power fails, it detects this and a battery supply switches in automatically.

Unfortunately, that battery provides DC power, so a built-in inverter has to convert this to AC. This is the weakness of the offline method: in between the power failing and the inverter cutting in there can be a slight but noticeable delay which can cause data corruption or loss. Because of this offline systems are never used in applications which are mission-critical.

Line-interactive

This can be best described as an offline unit with additional safe-guards. When the power fails, inertia alone will keep any motors on the same circuit spinning for a while – effectively turning them into tiny generators. They thus generate some power, which is fed back into the circuit and can confuse a UPS into believing the power is still on, fatally delaying the switch-over to battery reserve. To avoid this, an interactive UPS has a temporary energy buffer stored in a transformer, so that the computer sees no break in power.

Online

In this type of UPS, sometimes described as continuous online, the current is fed directly into a battery, and at the other side of this an inverter continuously provides power to the computer. With this system no charge reaches the battery when the power fails, but, until it runs down, the battery can still keep supplying the computer by way of the inverter. There is thus no break in the supply, and any noise or surges are automatically catered for. Online UPS systems are the most reliable, but also the most costly.

Specifications and Cost Calculations

One feature common to all types of UPS is known as the output waveform. Mains electricity, when plotted on a graph or shown on an oscilloscope, has a perfectly smooth – sinusoidal – wave which not every inverter can reproduce. The cheapest produce a square wave, looking more like the crenellations on a castle, while others reach the peaks and troughs of the wave via discrete steps, producing what is known as a stepped waveform.

According to the manufacturers whose inverters produce true sinusoidal output, anything less could affect the efficiency of the computer. They argue that, as this is what electronic components were designed to use, they are unlikely to work well with other waveforms. For anyone using an online UPS this is a point well worth considering, but for other types of UPS the case has yet to be proved conclusively. Certainly, for the few minutes of power being supplied just to close a system down, it is unlikely to make any difference.

There are in fact much more important factors to be taken into consideration. Chief amongst these is the power rating necessary if the UPS is to provide sufficient cover. Fortunately, this can be calculated easily, just by taking the volts (V) multiplied by the amps (A) for the equipment to be protected. Work this out for each item to be plugged into the UPS and add them all together. This final VA figure is then the minimum power rating for the UPS. The relevant figures are usually printed on the back of each device, and will always be listed in the accompanying documentation, so they can be easily found. (The only slight problem is that sometimes the wattage figure is listed, but that can be easily overcome: simply multiply the wattage by 1.4 to obtain the equivalent VA rating.)

Then remember the following:

Allow for any peripheral devices. Extras, like larger monitors or additional hard drives, can have a significant effect on the overall VA figure.

Allow for expansion. If the system is to be expanded or upgraded in the foreseeable future, use the VA figures for the new equipment, not the old. Why buy a UPS that could soon become unable to meet your needs?

Allow for overloads. Temporary overloads (also known as inrush currents) can be created when a disk drive or monitor is switched on, and these can exceed the UPS rating for a few seconds. The longer the UPS can withstand this overload, the better. If there is no overload capability built in, then the UPS will have to be oversized to cope.

The next factor to be considered is running costs. Here efficiency is the key: the higher the efficiency rating, the lower the running costs. This is straightforward enough – except that efficiency ratings vary with load. A line-interactive device generally has high efficiency at high loads and lower efficiency at low loads, while the reverse is true of an online unit. This is almost guaranteed to cause confusion, as the loading on a UPS is about 40%-50% for most of the time.

The best advice that can be given is to take the efficiency ratings for both full and half loads and use these to calculate the annual running costs. This can be done easily in a series of steps:

Input power   = Capacity (W) ÷ Efficiency
Operating power = Input power (W) – Output power (W)
Hourly cost   = Operating power × Unit price of electricity

The annual cost is therefore the hourly cost multiplied by the number of hours the device will be operational.

Purists can also add in such things as delivery and installation costs, maintenance contracts or the price of replacement batteries, which do add to the total expenditure but can be ignored for comparison purposes. If the whole point of calculating the total cost is to choose between the various UPS on the market, it can generally be assumed that maintenance contracts and such are roughly similar.

More problematic is the cost of air-conditioning. Every UPS generates heat, so having several in the same room could call for some kind of air-conditioning. If that exists already, then the extra cost involved in running a UPS could be debatable. On the other hand, if air-conditioning is there solely to cool the UPS, then its running costs will have to be included in the calculations of UPS costs. This can be done using the formula:

Hourly cost = Energy Efficiency Ratio × Unit price of electricity.

(The energy efficiency ratio is a figure quoted by all air-conditioning manufacturers. It is calculated from the ability of the unit to remove a certain number of British Thermal Units from a given area.)

Having worked through the costs it is possible that a UPS no longer seems such a cost-effective option. At the very least, plans to protect every piece of equipment might have to be scaled down. This is only to be expected. Like a fire-extinguisher, a UPS offers no quantifiable increase in productivity, and if data is backed up regularly (as it should be) the potential savings could be minimal. So, on the face of it, the UPS has very little to recommend it. Think again, though. Once the repair or replacement cost of any equipment that a UPS could save from damage is added to the equation, the figures start to move in the right direction.

Further savings come from another effect of power loss. The operating system of a PC normally keeps track of where all the files are on the hard disk, but in a power cut the information it was storing for its own housekeeping purposes will be lost. In non-technical terms, when the power returns the computer might not be able to find those files any more: the disk, as they say, will have been corrupted. If this happens to a large disk on a network file-server, not only will the network be down for some time to come, but an outside specialist may have to be called in, and his bill will come to a lot more than the price of a UPS.

Remember, too, that a file-server only rarely saves to disk immediately. Instead it keeps data in a temporary memory store until other requests are dealt with. Only then, when no other calls are being made on its processor, does it actually write to disk. This means that sudden power failure can cause the loss of a lot more data than can be easily replaced. And trying would cost money.

So a UPS can be a worthwhile investment. During an electrical storm or power failure it can easily pay for itself many times over. For companies struggling to justify the initial investment expenditure, the only advice that can be given is to take it step by step. Assign a priority level to each piece of equipment and start by protecting those with the highest priority, leaving the others until financial considerations allow for more. Needless to say, mission-critical devices should be protected immediately, as should network servers, for reasons already explained. Also high on the list should be backup devices. In fact organizations with a lot of data would do well to make sure that the UPS is capable of providing power for the full backup process, buying extra battery packs if need be. Given that problems so often strike at the worst possible moment, the thought of a power cut during backup should be the stuff of nightmares for the safety-conscious manager.

As for the rest of the equipment, one possible scale of priorities could be based on its value – always remembering that the key word is *value*, not price. A high-specification workstation complete with CAD package might be the most expensive piece of equipment in the building, but a lowly PC holding new sales orders or customer enquiries would be more valuable to the company. In short, look at the overall needs of the organization and then make a decision based on individual requirements.

On that basis a note of caution should be sounded about testing the UPS. Traditionally this is usually done by simply pulling out the plug connecting the UPS to the mains (imaginatively referred to as the plug-pull test). However, this is not necessarily a good indicator of future performance; in real-world conditions the presence of other electrical equipment can affect the results. During the plug-pull test this equipment remains operational, but during an actual power failure it obviously cuts out too. There is, therefore, a difference in the electrical characteristics of the circuit which, although slight, is still capable of increasing the response time by anywhere between twenty and fifty per cent. In other words, the time taken for a UPS to switch in during a genuine power cut could be as much as half as long again as during the plug-pull test. This is something to be seriously considered when systems are being evaluated.

Another consideration is the life of the battery. Replacement batteries are expensive, and yet their failure can fundamentally affect system reliability. Here the design of the UPS can make a major difference. The points to watch out for are:

Battery temperature. Battery life is affected by heat, so the UPS should be designed to keep the battery as cool as possible.

Battery charger design. The natural ageing process of the battery is arrested if it is kept under constant charge. Because of this it is essential that the UPS constantly charges the battery, even if the unit itself is switched off.

Battery voltage. All batteries are made up of a series of cells connected together. However, slight imperfections in manufacturing can cause some cells to take a larger percentage of the charging voltage than the others, which causes premature ageing of the cell and, consequently, of the battery. This means that a battery with a small number of large cells is preferable to one with a large number of small cells. The unit with the longest battery life is the unit with the lowest battery voltage.

Battery ripple current. Although batteries should be

constantly charged, inverting AC current to DC results in frequent interruptions to the charging process. This causes a ripple current which ages the battery. Here the design of the UPS is critical:

If the battery is placed between the charger and the inverter then it will be subjected to a ripple current.

If the battery is isolated from the inverter, by a diode for example, then there will be no ripple current.

In most cases the battery is the least reliable part of any UPS system. It is also the only part with a finite life span. This means that the battery's life span and the cost of replacements should be considered when systems are being evaluated. As ever, the better-designed systems are likely to have the longest battery life but will be more expensive. The only advice that can be offered is to shop around, do the calculations and choose whatever system suits the individual requirements.

5 Security Procedures

In 1995 the *Times* reported that an employee of the National Westminster Bank had tried to transfer £31 million into a Swiss account using a stolen computer password. The attempt apparently failed because the receiving bank, Credit Suisse of Zurich, refused to accept the transfer on the grounds that it was in excess of trading limits agreed between the two banks. The alarm was therefore raised, and the employee was caught when it was remembered that on the day of the transfer he had been in a part of the NatWest building in Islington for which he had no authorization.

Just another story in a newspaper perhaps, but it raises questions relevant to all computer-users. For the moment, forget the issue of the stolen password (which is dealt with later). Instead consider how that employee was allowed access to a part of the building for which he had no authorization, and why, although he was seen, no one challenged him. The answer – the only possible answer – is that security procedures were ignored. The incident provides a dramatic demonstration of how easily this can happen, and what the results can be.

To put that in perspective, not every company would be even worth £31 million, far less have it in cash. Even so, the principles involved still apply. To a smaller business the cost of a security breach could well represent a higher proportion of its turnover than that £31m did to a major bank. And, whereas the Bank of England would step in to save a major bank from collapse, no bank would do the same for any other company. Anyone operating without that kind of safety-net had best look to their own security procedures, therefore.

In practice this means such simple, common-sense precautions as not leaving a reception area unattended during lunch breaks, or segregating duties so that, for example, the person who raises purchase orders is not the person who authorizes payment. Building security into the system, in other words. This is nothing an averagely competent manager would even need to think about – until computers enter the equation. At that point everything changes, because laying down security procedures is no longer enough – they must also be strictly maintained.

British Telecom is one of the government's chief advisers on computer security. It even worked alongside the DTI in drawing up standard guidelines. Yet the *Independent* reported in 1994 that even temporary BT staff were given access to the confidential addresses and telephone numbers of the intelligence services, cabinet ministers and the Royal family. The right guidelines were in place; it was just that no one was following them.

Management's Role

The most surprising aspect of security breaches is that companies are prepared to risk so much when security can be maintained so easily, and at no extra cost. All it takes is the application of a few basic principles.

The first of these is the golden rule of security: involve senior management. As with the contingency plan, unless senior managers are prepared to give their full support, everything else falls apart. Unless security is company-wide, it is non-existent.

That has to be understood from the beginning. Top executives have to be involved because it means that high-level managers must face the same disciplinary process as low-level clerks.

Throughout the country there are examples of managers going unpunished for security lapses that would cost someone else their job. This perhaps, helps to explain why most firms have such weak security. Once someone is seen to flout the rules without penalty, those rules become unenforceable and are ignored. Soon all security procedures start to break down, and any attempt to reimpose them will be met with outright hostility. If that reimposition results in someone being sacked for a crime no worse than the manager committed without being punished, then this could even lead to a case of unfair dismissal.

Be warned and be prepared. There is no such thing as partial security.

To keep all procedures in place, the recommended practice is to form a Security Committee. Like the Safety Committee, this would meet regularly both to discuss ways of improving security and to highlight any breaches. Any lapses in security should be immediately reported to one of its members, just as safety lapses are reported to the Safety Committee. (At this juncture it is worth pointing out that failing to report a security breach is as bad as committing it – both leave the organization exposed.)

As for the composition of the committee, two groups should be excluded: security personnel and contingency planners. Security officers tend to be ex-policemen with little or no computer training. If knowledge of the system is needed to break into it, then only people with an equal knowledge can protect it; security officers usually lack such specific expertise. A contingency planner might possess the desired expertise, but, if such a person were a member of the Security Committee, should they ever leave, the company would lose a disaster-recovery expert and a security expert at the same time. Keeping the two functions separate not only removes that risk, it also spreads the workload.

65

The IT Department could be represented, but not exclusively – and not necessarily at all. During the investigation of a security breach the department's help will be needed, if only to produce the audit logs (a list of who accessed what files from which terminal and when). Beyond that, it helps if its members are kept in the background in favour of the actual computer-users. That way the message is clearly sent that security is the responsibility of everyone, not just the technical whizz-kids.

Policy Guidelines

Unfortunately, there is a lot more to security than just locked doors. Where computers are concerned, other factors have to be taken into consideration. Some measures will be beyond the needs of individual companies, whereas other companies will need a complete range of precautions; it all depends on the nature of the organization and the confidentiality of its data. In a general work such as this, all that can be offered is a set of guidelines and points to consider.

Make it Easy to Report Suspicious Activity

If there is an easy way for staff to report possible break-in attempts, whether physical intrusions or efforts by hackers breaking into the computer system, then there is a good chance that such attempts will be reported. This can only be good for the company in the long term. Never complain about time wasted on false alarms, therefore – instead see it as proof that staff members are being properly vigilant, for which they should be praised.

Seal Off the Data – Not the Staff

Most high-security areas are physically partitioned off from the rest of the company. Unfortunately, so too are its staff – who, being human, naturally want to mix with everyone on the outside. Whether to exchange gossip, pay their share of the pools or lottery syndicate, or even to further an office romance, people on opposite sides of the security fence will want to talk to each other, and in the process security is wrecked. An office junior calls to collect the tea money, someone else 'just pops in' to tell the story about Mr Smith and his secretary – all this is part of the daily routine found in any office. However, it means that the security area rapidly becomes non-existent, because, when one or two can walk in unchallenged, others will inevitably follow. Soon anyone who feels like it will walk through, and it will all be perfectly innocent – most of the time.

A much safer proposition is to split the work of the staff inside the restricted area into that which is confidential and that which is not; this is something which can be done even in the most sensitive establishments. Confidential work is obviously carried out in the restricted area. Non-confidential work can be done in an area immediately outside it, and here anyone can stop by to talk, collect names for the works outing or whatever other socializing is done in the rest of the company. No data is at risk, the staff can mix as freely as they want, but no one has an excuse for going inside the high-security area. (And in this case 'no one' includes the people who deliver office supplies; they, too, can be kept out, simply by making them deliver to the less secure area.) This arrangement has the added bonus that it also means that only people actually working on sensitive data will be in the secure zone, restricting access to confidential material still further.

Beware the Smoking Area

The importance of this principle was shown during the investigation into the activities of CIA spy Aldrich Ames. Many organizations now operating a No Smoking policy, and those who still smoke are forced together into a designated smoking area, where inevitably they talk shop. Since they all share the common bond of being 'outcasts', the normal security restrictions are ignored, and an alert spy can pick up a great deal of valuable information. In the case of Aldrich Ames, no actual secrets were given away, but he did discover what topics were currently interesting the CIA and where he should look to find out more. In more commercial environments things like new product launches, major problems or forthcoming changes to the company structure could all be leaked out with potentially fatal consequences.

Since separate smoking areas for staff on different grades or from different departments are impractical the only real solution is to warn employees with, perhaps, a poster in the smoking area of the 'Loose Lips Sinks Ships' variety.

Control Security Classifications

There are two separate issues here: the way files are classified, and the range of classifications available. Taking them in that order, if too many files are designated as secret, then all respect for the system is lost. Files that should be kept under lock and key are left lying on desks, usually amongst files full of trivia which have the same security classification. Security then becomes not just something to be ignored, but something much worse: a laughing matter, a joke. That may sound impossible, and yet of all the possible lapses in security this is the easiest to fall into.

According to classical management theory, the desire for status is a powerful motivating force. In security terms this means individuals will always want to prove or improve their apparent status within an organization by having all their work marked 'Secret', or at the very least 'Confidential'. If there are several people of like mind (and they can be found in any organization), then the classification of files spirals rapidly upwards. A memo is sent marked 'Confidential'; to prove superiority, the recipient sends a reply marked 'Secret'; this leads someone else to send their memo as 'Top Secret' – and so the cycle continues, until all files are high security and no one believes any of it. (In the Ministry of Defence this once reached the point where even the menu in the staff restaurant was a classified document!) Eventually the entire process becomes a standing joke within the organization and the system's disrepute leads inevitably to lapses of security.

Fortunately the problem is easy to spot – memos and reports have a higher security rating than they deserve – although preventing it is harder. Education and the occasional harsh word can help, but the easiest solution of all is to keep the number of security grades to an absolute minimum. In any organization no more than four should be used:

Open: No security designation whatsoever.

Confidential: For material which, if disclosed, could harm the organization or benefit a rival.

Restricted: For material limited only to named individuals.

Registered: For the most sensitive of all material. Not only is this restricted to named individuals, they must also sign for it and accept total responsibility for what happens to it while in their possession.

These four grades cover all security requirements, and the gap between them is large enough for it to become immediately obvious if anyone is misusing the system. As long as the definitions are known and understood, a properly monitored staff will be forced into adopting the correct procedures. (In this particular context, of course, 'properly monitored' means, watch out for the restaurant menu arriving by registered post.)

No one can eradicate the desire for status. The best that can be done is to channel it into other, more productive directions and to restrict the number of security classifications available. Only the Pentagon needs files marked 'Above Top Secret'.

Be Careful How Disks Are Labelled

Even the most honest employee will want a copy of a disk or file marked 'Proposed Redundancies'. Similarly, key accounts or marketing information will be at risk from those who are less than honest. Since files or disks must be labelled, a simple, no-cost security measure is to always use innocuous-sounding titles. For example a disk could be labelled 'notes for meeting on Friday 21st'. That meeting might well be held to discuss proposed redundancies, but, since no one could tell that by reading the label, the casual thief or inquisitive employee is more likely to ignore it.

Protect Obsolete Data

Data that is no longer needed but is still sensitive must be destroyed. That includes disks, tapes and cartridges as well as paper. Magnetic media can be reused, so more than just deleting the files is necessary (software exists to undelete them). At the very least the disks should be reformatted. However, it should always be remembered that the software package which can undelete files will also offer the facility to unformat a disk, as a means of data recovery. Fortunately, software also exists to wipe out data beyond hope of recovery, and this is one of the options that should be used.

However, if destruction is the chosen alternative, then specialist companies do exist to cater for this, although not all of them have their own shredding facilities. Sometimes this will be subcontracted, which puts sensitive data at further risk. This is something that should be checked before a contract is placed. Also be sure that the data will not be needed again. Once a disk has been chopped into tiny pieces there is no way back.

Be Wary of Faxes and Modems

Information no longer has to be physically carried out of the building; nowadays it can be sent electronically by fax or modem. In fact this was how Iraq acquired a good part of its nuclear technology, despite the best efforts of the CIA, MI6 and several atomic regulatory commissions. That fact demonstrates just how easy data theft is, and how dangerous. Fortunately there are ways of reducing the risk.

With faxes a log should be kept of all calls made. This should include: the fax numbers, the names of both recipient and sender, what was sent and why. Depending on circumstances, it might even be worth inspecting the log on a regular basis for any unusual entries. Failing that, the mere fact of its existence should act as a deterrent to anyone considering illegal activity.

With modems the situation is different. If communications packages are installed on a computer, the software should be configured so that only a predetermined list of telephone numbers is available. The daily routine is in no way affected, but users are barred from making any other calls.

Use Screen-Savers

Confidential data left on an unattended computer practically invites snooping. While in theory it is possible to issue directives forbidding this, in practice it very rarely happens. Rather than close down an application and log out of a system beforehand (and then have to reverse the process afterwards), all for the sake of a quick trip to the toilet or coffee machine, a user will more likely leave the application running – only to be delayed on the way back. Alternatively, a supervisor might be called to answer a simple query that turns into something much more time-consuming. There are any number of reasons why a machine could be left unattended, and to expect that staff will conscientiously close down the system each and every time they leave their terminal is to ask too much of human nature. A much safer option is to install screen-savers, which automatically blank the screen after a preset interval.

If a password option is available with the screen-saver use that too, purely as a safeguard. In this one instance the password does not have to be kept secure. It works like this. The person standing next to a computer might be snooping, or they might have a good reason for being there. The person standing next to a computer with its screen-saver deactivated might be snooping, or they may have accidentally moved the mouse (which is all it takes to restore the screen). But the person who disables the screen-saver using the password is a thief.

Remember, though, that screen-savers are not secure. Even if the password is unknown, they can be bypassed simply by switching the computer off and then back on again. If this is too much of a security risk to run, it might be worth considering a piece of software called Screen-saver Enhancer (SSE) which is available as shareware. Amongst other things, this allows the screen-saver to be activated immediately, without the usual waiting period. Just as importantly, it can also activate a screen-saver as soon as Windows starts up, thus preventing the password system from being by-passed.

Alternatively for those not too worried about making changes to the system settings, a DIY method is possible. First take a text editor (like Notepad) and use it to edit the file WIN.INI so that the line 'programs com exe bat pif' now reads 'programs com exe bat pif scr'. After that not very difficult job, restart Windows, so the alteration can take effect, and a screen-saver can then be treated just like any other program: assign it an icon, create a shortcut key – or even drag it into the Startup Group, so it will activate as soon as the computer is switched on. Just remember that in the command line (found by choosing Properties from the File menu) the name of the screen-saver should be followed by '/s'. For example, the Starfield command line would be 'SSSTARS.SCR/S'. In fact any file with the extension .SCR can be used, and, if the password options are enabled, not even switching the machine off and then back on again will work.

Be Suspicious of Demonstrations

This belongs in the category of strange, but true. A salesman could call, ostensibly to demonstrate a new piece of software, but actually to steal. On the floppy disk or disks supposedly carrying the demonstration software another program is hidden. This copies data files from the hard drive to the floppy, then, as a precaution, deletes them (so that, even if that disk is checked by security, it will show nothing out of the ordinary, for the files have all been deleted). Later a standard, commercially available package is used to undelete the files on the disk, and confidential data falls into the hands of a thief. A variation on the same theme is to leave a program installed on the hard drive to monitor all keypresses. After a few days the 'salesman' returns, at which time he transfers this information (which will include any passwords entered into the computer) to another floppy disk, which he then takes away with him.

This may sound fantastic, almost science fiction, but in one documented instance it happened, and the victim was the police force. Fortunately, the perpetrator was a security consultant interested only in making a point, so no harm was done. The point that consultant was trying to make is that such software is freely available on the Internet, and anyone interested in data theft could have a copy. It is even possible that the only reason so few cases of data theft are reported is because this method is virtually undetectable.

Against this kind of attack there can only be one line of defence. Do not allow software to be demonstrated on a computer holding confidential information. Also, keep the demonstration well clear of any networks; they can be searched just as easily as a local hard drive.

If all this is too James Bond, remember that another, low-tech, threat also exists. The salesman might just be there to find out what kind of security procedures are in force.

Always Prosecute

When supermarkets prosecute shoplifters for even the most trivial offence, they do it to warn anyone else who might be tempted. As they long ago discovered, the only true deterrent is the threat of punishment, and what works for supermarkets works for any other company. The theft of data is as much a crime as the theft of property, and anyone caught should be prosecuted.

A common reaction from some managers is that to prosecute would embarrass the company; it would make public any gaps in its security. Perhaps this goes without saying, but, all the same, this is the voice of self-interest speaking. What those managers really mean is it would embarrass *them*. Other companies would be taking no pleasure in the news, nor would they reap any commercial benefit – not from a company who has just proved its ability to catch data thieves. More likely those companies would be too busy reviewing their own, probably inadequate, security systems.

To take the counter-argument one step further, the embarrassment factor means that hacking incidents usually go unreported. As a result, the police have no idea of the scale of the problem, and are therefore unable to allocate sufficient resources. Because of this, prosecutions are rare – so no-one bothers to report any incidents. Break this chicken-and-egg cycle! Report the matter to the police – and if the local constabulary are unable to respond, go direct to the Computer Crime Unit at Scotland Yard.

As the Roman military writer Vegetius said, 'let him who desires peace, prepare for war'. Only by being constantly alert to the dangers can they be prevented; conversely, ignoring the threat means it will come true. Complacency is the real enemy. Only that allows procedures to fall into disuse and systems to fall into disrepair; only that makes the organization vulnerable.

The key to good security is not just system maintenance, being alert to potential loopholes is equally important. A good example of this can be found in the *Information Security Breaches Survey 1996*. One of its case studies showed a loophole that involved the fact that word-processing software automatically creates backup files, so that when a file is saved to disk another copy of it is made. As a way of preventing data loss the idea is obviously sound, but, as one unfortunate company discovered, it also has security implications. In this case, although the main files were secure, an enterprising employee was able to access those forgotten backup files, and in the process created a massive security breach.

The moral of the story is that systems are not always as secure as they look. Even security experts admit there is no such thing as a totally safe organization. Changes to the system or to its software will always create fresh loopholes for an alert mind to spot. Just be certain that the person who finds them is there to protect, not to steal.

6   Passwords

Passwords are probably the best known, the most widely used and, potentially, the least reliable of all available security measures. At their best they provide a highly effective barrier between sensitive data and prying eyes; at their worst they can have all the security potential of a door with the key still in the lock. No matter who uses it, if the right password is used the system will be opened. That, in a nutshell, is the weakness. Once a password is known, it becomes a liability to the organization relying on it.

Added to that is the problem of actually creating a password, and then repeating the process every time it has to be changed. Doing it once can be difficult; do it any more than that and it starts to become a nightmare. When Barclays Bank moved to a distributed computing environment (PCs on desks), it found that one particular manager had to remember no fewer than forty. Fairly obviously, at that kind of level security is more of a problem than a solution, but even at lower levels the principle still applies. If too many passwords are needed, the temptation is strong to use just one and apply it everywhere, effectively reducing its protective value.

The first point, therefore, has to be, restrict the number of passwords. Too many and the system falls apart under its own weight.

Creating and Memorizing Passwords

Creating passwords is not a simple matter. There is a long list of things to avoid, but very little on how to do it. There is a very good reason for this: if the process *could* be reduced to a simple formula, then a thief could follow the same formula to arrive at the same password. For that reason alone, password creation has to be a very idiosyncratic affair. Even so there are ways of making it easier.

Any random collection of characters will do to create a password, but the problem lies in remembering it afterwards. One trick is to use an acronym – for example, WALOD could stand for 'What A Lot Of Data'. This has the advantage of being easy to remember, but combines it with the disadvantage of being easy to penetrate. Unfortunately, if a thief spots the complete phrase written down (and passwords usually *are* written down, despite the practice being frowned on) then the password becomes obvious in seconds flat. To avoid this, use more than just the first letter. In this way NESALLDS could stand for 'New Sales Leads'. A bit harder to remember, but a lot more secure (assuming the phrase is written down without the relevant letters being highlighted).

Another method is to borrow a trick from the cryptic crossword compilers and hide the word inside another phrase – so WASP could be found from 'New as Pin'. If the phrase is longer, so much the better. Better still is to make sure the password bears absolutely no relevance to the data being protected. Why give a potential thief any clues?

Although tricks like these can be used to good effect, always remember they are only secure when no one knows what to look out for. Once it becomes generally realized that a manager always uses a cryptic clue, for example, the password is so easy to work out as to be almost public knowledge. The best system of all is to use a variety of methods and follow a random pattern in selecting which one to apply.

There is still a lot more to the business of password creation, but one point stands out above all others: do not under any circumstances pin passwords to the notice board. Many companies still do this, and it makes about as much sense as trusting physical security to a door with no lock. Some form of memory aid – kept privately and in a form incomprehensible to others – is acceptable (just), but further than that no one should go.

If there is a genuine problem in remembering a password then, under certain conditions, it could be shared with a colleague on the same security level. That way, what one forgets the other might remember. The chances are both will have access to the self-same files (or, at the very least, those with the same security rating), so the risk of a security breach is only slight, whereas the benefits could be immeasurable. However, if this is to be done the ground rules must be laid down first.

Share with one, and one only. Every time a password is shared, the risk of accidental disclosure increases, as does the number of people with access to private files. Swapping passwords with one other person can be a viable alternative to the written note, but share with more and the risks become unacceptable.

Make the arrangement formal. A written record should be kept of who is sharing passwords with whom, but not, repeat not, the password itself. That way, if data is stolen or altered, the innocent party has an alibi. If passwords are swapped informally, the holder of that data has no way of proving that anyone else had access to it.

Keep to the same partner. If everyone constantly changes the person they swap passwords with, keeping the formal record up to date becomes a major job – which is another way of saying it will be ignored.

Respect confidentiality. Shouting a password from one side of the office to another is only marginally better than pinning it to a notice board. If a password is asked for, make sure no one else can overhear it being passed on.

It has to be said not everyone is in favour of password swaps, and there *are* inherent risks involved, but between responsible members of staff it could perform a valuable function as an alternative to writing anything down. Needless to say, anyone involved in a swapping arrangement who then writes down both passwords is a danger to the organization and should be treated as such – and the treatment should be backed up with disciplinary measures. The whole point of the exercise is to exchange the potential risk of a written password for the much more controllable risk of sharing it with someone else – and even then only as a last resort. The best method of all is to just remember the password without need of help.

Moving on from there, a great many other traps also exist, any one of which could compromise system security and so must be avoided. Here are some tips.

Avoid Using Familiar Names

It is estimated that a full eighty per cent of all security threats come from within the organization. This implies that anyone trying to break into a system may already know the password-holder – at least to the extent of knowing their outside interests and the names of their immediate family. Therefore, none of this information should be used as the basis for a password.

The names of husbands, wives, sons or daughters are the first thing any potential thief would try – closely followed by the names of footballers, movies or whatever else the password-holder is interested in. It might seem like a good idea to use familiar names, because they are easy to remember, but the temptation must be resisted. Otherwise anyone with a knowledge of the password-holder need only try out a very limited range of options, one of which will allow access to the system.

Avoid Single, Proper, Words

There now exists a type of electronic 'dictionary' which a thief can use to search automatically for the right password. Using dedicated software, each entry in the dictionary is matched against the password request and, since these dictionaries can hold anything up to 250,000 entries, the chances are high that a single-word password will be found. The only defence against this is to use either more than one word or a made-up nonsense word.

Even for organizations where the system is unlikely to be attacked by anything so hi-tech, this advice still holds good, because a single, proper, word can more easily be guessed. Two words are just as easy to remember, but infinitely harder to penetrate.

Use Both Upper and Lower Case

Most password software is what is known as case-sensitive, which means that, say, 'SECURE' would register as a different word from 'secure', or even 'Secure'. Intelligently applied, this feature can be used to increase the number of combinations any thief has to search through. Do not start with a capital letter and then revert to lower case throughout. Instead, use a mixture of both at any time. A capital letter in the midDle of a word is both hArder to predict and haRder to detect.

Use More Than Just Letters

There is no law to say that passwords must consist only of letters of the alphabet. Numbers can be used too, either by themselves (but not in such an obvious sequence as, say, 123456) or in combination with letters. When used properly, these alphanumeric codes can be highly effective in increasing the range of possible permutations, although if used badly they can be extremely dangerous.

If a manager is known to be using the password 'DATA1', for example, how long would it take a thief to work out that subsequent passwords are most likely to be 'DATA2', 'DATA3' and so on. However the remedy for this is as obvious as the danger: never number passwords consecutively. Whether a sequence involves the next number, the next odd number or even the next prime number, the point is a pattern exists which could be discovered and then used to defeat the system.

Alphanumeric combinations can also be used to spell a word in much the same way as personalized number plates on cars, but such combinations should still be treated with caution. Once a thief knows the relevant word everything else is very easy to work out.

In much the same way other keyboard characters can also be used. Symbols such as £, &, or # can equally add to the number of available permutations although the same warnings still apply. If they are used to spell a word or phrase (like Mr_10%) that word or phrase could be guessed, making the system vulnerable.

Finally do not just change the order of these characters to generate a new password. For example ABCDE$, ABCD$E and ABC$DE might all be accepted by the computer as different passwords, but literally anyone could guess what the next new password would be. There will always be people trying to guess other people's passwords, so why make it easy for them?

Using Passwords

Refuse to Enter a Password if Anyone is Watching

Although a professional typist could enter a password too fast for anyone else to see, most managers lack such advanced keyboard skills. Their one-finger style of text entry makes it almost childishly simple for a bystander to see what their password is. This raises the unspoken (and unpleasant) question: is that colleague standing there innocently, or is there a more sinister motive involved?

Such a question can be neither asked nor answered; even thinking it breeds the kind of suspicion that can destroy good working relationships. So avoid the problem at its source. As a matter of courtesy move away while someone else enters their password, and insist they do the same for you. It costs nothing, it increases security and it prevents the office atmosphere from becoming too corrosive – so there can be no excuse for not doing it.

Change Passwords Regularly

Even with the best safeguards imaginable, a long-standing password will eventually become known to everyone. This is only to be expected, so it makes sense to change passwords regularly. Once a month is the usual interval recommended; any longer than that and the benefits of keeping an existing, easily remembered, password begin to be outweighed by the risk of it becoming generally known.

Additionally, the software should prevent just two passwords being used alternately – known as flip-flopping. The recommended practice is for at least six months to pass before any password is reused; if the period is any shorter, a vigilant but not necessarily honest employee might start to notice a pattern emerging. Needless to say, not using *any* password twice is still the safest option.

Ban Competitions

Competitions can develop between users over who has the best, strangest, or even the most obscene, password. This means everyone gets to know every other password. People without passwords of their own could overhear, or a hacker who knew the theme of the competition (X-Files, football, etc.) would at the very least have a limited range of guesses to make before hitting on the right one. These competitions should be banned.

When Staff Leave Always Change the Passwords

From a security point of view there is no such thing as a good reason for staff to leave. Those sacked or made redundant will have a grievance and might want to strike back at the company; those going on maternity leave could be under financial pressure; even those leaving to take up another job could have hidden motives (it is worth asking what dissatisfaction or disaffection drove them to look for another job in the first place). There is even the possibility that someone else has their password and can use it to access confidential files, knowing that suspicion will fall on the employee who has just left.

Even if everyone is scrupulously honest, it still makes sense to change any common passwords and remove from the system any that were specific to a particular person. To do otherwise leaves the company vulnerable for no good reason, which is bad security – and an almost criminal lack of common sense.

System Considerations

Prohibit Multiple Log-ins

If two people are using the same password then one of them is using it illegally. More than one log-on on the same password must be prevented even if it means the legitimate user is locked out – and the system manager must be alerted.

In most cases the thief is a fellow worker who keeps the same office hours, and this makes data theft by this means difficult, although not impossible. So the thief is forced either to stay late or to come in early – activities which have to be explained, and which will be recorded in the security log. In other words, a deterrent is there.

Avoid Systems With Password-recovery Options

Some companies market security software with the added 'bonus' that if a password is lost or forgotten the system can still be accessed to recover it. Do not use this software. In security parlance it means the system has a 'back door': another, hidden, password known only to the software company.

Any organization with a system like this is reliant not only on its own safeguards, but also those of an outside company. That company is staffed by people with no reason to feel any particular loyalty towards the organization whose data is at risk – nor, if they are sacked, made redundant or just passed over for promotion, do they necessarily have any feelings of loyalty towards their own employer.

Tempting as it might be to have this kind of option as a safety fall-back, there are better ways of making sure that passwords are neither lost nor forgotten – and none of them carry the same level of risk.

Use System-Manager Passwords for System-Manager Tasks Only

On a network the System Manager will have a secondary, extremely wide-ranging, password to use when carrying out network maintenance. As this allows unlimited access to the network, it should be used only for that maintenance. For day-to-day routine work only the normal user-level passwords should be used. It is possible for the log-in program to be altered so that it stores any passwords used, to be revealed later; a dedicated hacker would know this. While it might be bad enough for such a person to have user-level passwords, access to the system-manager password could prove disastrous.

In many ways passwords represent not only the best but also the worst of all security systems. It takes time and effort to create and remember them, and they come between workers and their jobs, making those jobs much more difficult to do. Passwords do not increase productivity levels or generate extra business, nor do they make existing customers any more likely to keep doing business with the company. In short, like all security systems, they take time, cost money and add nothing to the business. Yet, again like all security systems, not having them could wipe out the company. The trick is to find the right balance between security and convenience.

Passwords and Data Categories

As always in this life, that can only be achieved through planning and careful preparation. This begins with separating the corporate date into clearly recognizable categories – something like the following:

Open: Data with no commercial value outside the organization.

Confidential: Sensitive data which must be kept secure.

Personal: Data kept by an individual manager and secured by a personal, unique password.

Project: Short-term projects which by their nature must be kept secure.

Depending on the nature of the organization, the exact details may vary, but probably not by too much. Most data should fit into one of these categories. Levels of security can then be assigned to the categories.

Open

This is for data which may be vital to the company but is of no interest to the outside world. For example, the status of a particular order being processed through the system is important only to the company. Competitors might like to know the frequency of those orders and the prices being charged, but knowing the delivery date of a particular order is unlikely to affect the share price much.

Any form of security at this level is pointless. Password protection will prevent staff from doing their jobs and needlessly add to the burden of anyone with other passwords to remember.

Confidential

For commercial or legal reasons, some data must be kept secure – so protect it. Password protection at this level can be highly effective, but not if the system is abused. As with the classification of documents any tendency to upgrade commercially valueless information must be strongly resisted; otherwise the system becomes simultaneously overloaded and brought into disrepute. Worse still, anyone needing access to data that has been classified at too high a level must also be given access to information which is genuinely confidential.

Personal

Anyone in a position of authority might have data relating to the staff under their control, or which has to be kept away from the staff under their control. Either way, this should be protected by a separate password.

Project

From time to time people will be assigned to short-term projects which will usually need to be kept secure, and the best way of doing that is to give it a separate password.

If the logic of all this is followed, then it becomes obvious that good security can be achieved by using just two passwords, with a third for occasional use only. As most experts agree, this is the most anyone can be reasonably expected to cope with. Asking staff to remember more will most likely result in written notes being kept, with a consequent reduction in security.

It might be that someone is involved in several projects, and therefore needs to know a great many passwords. If so, a complete evaluation of the organization might prove to be a wiser move; it is worth asking how much of a contribution anyone could make if their time is spread too thinly. Either way, the initial premise holds good: passwords are there to protect data not to make working life impossible.

Passwords should make life impossible for the thief – which means applying more than just common sense to choosing them. *The Hacker's Handbook* (which does exist) lists the most commonly found passwords:

HELP	OPERATIONS
TEST	AID
TESTER	DISPLAY
SYSTEM	CALL
SYSTEM MANAGER	TERMINAL
SYSMAN	EXTERNAL
SYSOP	REMOTE
ENGINEER	CHECK
OPS	NET

CENTRAL	NETWORK
DEMO	PHONE
DEMONSTRATION	FRED

Perhaps it goes without saying, but any organization using these should change them immediately!

Also to be changed are any standard passwords supplied with the software package itself. Usually this will be something simple like LETMEIN. Such passwords are there only to enable the system to be installed, not to provide security. Hackers will know them, and try them first. To make matters worse, the password will be printed on the documentation accompanying the software, making it freely available to anyone who feels like reading the manual.

Another possible problem is that some software automatically creates its own passwords, in order to give it access to the system (e.g. backup software). Usually these passwords give it full supervisor rights and privileges. However, the software manufacturers always use the same passwords, and these are now well known (and freely traded over the Internet). Any software which is configured to run automatically – and so needs the kind of access which can only come from having its own password – should therefore be treated with care. Check with the manufacturer; ask about these hidden passwords, see if they can be changed to something non-standard (and unknown to the hacking community), and restrict such software's privileges to the barest minimum.

To summarize: passwords have no loyalty and serve any master. Keeping them secure is as important as keeping a door key out of the wrong hands.

7 File Encryption

Passwords can provide a great deal of security, but they also have their weaknesses: not least the way they can be defeated by commercially available data-recovery software. This works by taking information directly from the hard disk, by-passing the normal routines, so the dangers are obvious. Unfortunately this type of software is just too useful to make banning it from the site a viable option. There will always be times when data recovery or some kind of file fixing is needed. That being the case, security-conscious managers should at the very least be careful about who has a copy of this software, and they should never allow it to be duplicated (apart from being illegal, this also represents a massive security risk).

Even so, precautions like these only work if the computer is still under the control of the organization that owns it. If the computer is stolen the data on it is vulnerable. To make matters worse, the increasing popularity of portable computers is making theft a growing problem, as witness the incident in 1991 when an RAF Wing Commander had his laptop stolen, complete with the Allied plans for the Gulf War. How he came to be allowed out of the Ministry of Defence with such valuable information falls into the category of security procedures (or lack of them), but the incident does illustrate the fact that nowadays computers can be stolen very easily. (It is also an interesting reflection that, if Iraqi agents had been involved, the laptop could have been connected to a modem and its entire contents downloaded to Baghdad before the Wing Commander even knew it had been stolen.)

In a world where theft is a possibility (and theft always *is* a possibility), the only way to be truly safe is to use some form of file-encryption program. Then, even if the computer is stolen, the information stored on it will still be safe, because it is stored in an unbreakable code – a cypher impossible to crack without the key.

File encryption is likely to be a highly controversial issue for a long time to come. The problem is that encoding systems are now so sophisticated as to make them literally unbreakable. This makes them a major headache for the law-enforcement agencies, which are increasingly reliant on wire-tapping and computer information in the fight against organized crime, drug dealers and terrorists. As they see it, when they lose the ability to read a computer file they lose a valuable weapon. For this reason, the Americans at least are insisting on strict regulation of the software, including 'back doors' which they alone can open.

Reasonable as that sounds, various civil liberties organizations see the matter differently; to them, any government attempt to monitor the individual is a sinister development. It has to be said that the experts and the computer industry are on the side of the libertarians on this issue, albeit for different reasons. The experts oppose any idea of a back door on principle: once a weakness exists, and is known to exist, it will eventually be found and exploited. The industry, on the other hand, has more fundamental objections. It points out no one outside the USA would buy a security system knowing that it could be opened by the American Government – because, while the FBI, operating within the USA, might wait until the US courts gave their permission, the CIA, acting in foreign countries, would be unlikely to show the same restraint.

In Europe the situation is, if anything, even more confused – to the point where a common standard is unlikely to appear in the near future. France, for example, follows the same hard line as America and classes encryption software as munitions, subject to the same export regulations as guns, bombs or missiles. (In fact to use an encryption device in France requires the direct authorization of the Prime Minister.) By contrast, in Germany there is no legal restriction even on the domestic use of cryptography, and the encryption of data sent over the Internet is recommended at the highest level. As the stance taken by such major European countries could not be more different this does illustrate the scale of the problem caused by file encryption – especially as all European laws are supposed to be moving towards uniformity.

In Britain the situation is currently undefined. At the beginning of 1997 the then Conservative Government issued a consultation paper outlining its proposals for the licensing of Trusted Third Parties. (A Trusted Third Party or TTP is an organization which also holds a software key to a particular computer system. Each company, or individual, who uses file encryption gives a copy of their password to the TTP. Under normal circumstances this password is held securely, but if a government or law enforcement agency asks the password is handed over so they can read the encrypted files, a process known as Key-Escrow.) Despite the change of government this process is still continuing so that on 18-6-1997 John Battle MP the Minister for Industry, Energy, Science and Technology could refer to the consultation document in the House of Commons when, in answer to a written question, he replied that an analysis of this was underway. No time scale was given either for this analysis to be completed or for any future legislation.

However, or whenever, the differing national standards are resolved it is likely to be in line with a series of recommendations published in September 1995 by the Council of Europe snappily entitled 'Draft Recommendation No. R(95) Concerning Problems of Procedural Law Connected with Information Technology'.

This states that the needs of law-enforcement agencies are superior to the needs of the public at large, and that the authorization to search suspect premises should also include an authorization to search computer systems. While legislation along these lines would be welcomed by the various law-enforcement agencies in practice it is not likely to be that straightforward. As no government would cede either its secrets or its sovereignty to the kind of trans-national organization the system would require there is obviously a lot of negotiation still to be done.

How all this will be resolved, if it is resolved, will be very much a matter for the courts. However, by taking an interest in encryption systems, the various government agencies have at least defined the levels of security which each package might be expected to give. The US Department of Defense has evaluated computer systems against its Trusted Computer Systems Evaluation Criteria (TSEC) – also known as the Orange Book. This defines several categories which are often referred to by software manufacturers.

D: Minimal protection.

C1: File and directory read/write protection and user log-in authentication procedures. An audit log is not available.

C2: An audit log is provided, plus extra protection on the most important system files.

B1: Multi-level security is available, so that confidential files can be kept separate from those that are secret. Also included is access control, so that a user cannot change permissions on files or directories.

B2: Every file is labelled according to its security classification.

B3: Hardware security. Computers can only be connected through trusted cables, to prevent the lines being trapped.

A1: Not only must the design be subjected to rigorous mathematical testing, the equipment itself must be guarded in transit to prevent unauthorized tampering.

As ever, America and Europe have differing standards, which explains why the Information Technology Security Evaluation Criteria (ITSEC) was jointly published by Britain, France, Germany and Holland. This examines the security function against a scale of E0 (inadequate confidence), E1 (minimal confidence) through to E6 (highest confidence), with E3 roughly equating to the American B1 standard. Anything more than the E3 or B1 security ratings tends to be more for military applications rather than commercial use.

The plus side of this confusion is that the fact that government agencies are worried shows that the software is more than good enough for a commercial environment. Any system can therefore be bought with confidence, although naturally there is more than one way to skin this particular cat; there are, in fact, several systems on the market. Before they can be explained, however, the concept of a key must be explained.

Keys

Substitution

The world's first cipher is attributed to Julius Caesar. A substitution system, this simply substitutes for each letter the letter that comes three places after it in the alphabet: A becomes D, B becomes E, and so on. In this case the key was 3, because that was the number of places each letter moved. Obviously the key could be 4, 5 or any other number up to 25, and each one would change the way the message was encrypted. Two thousand years ago that might have been a good system, but, with only 26 possible numbers, a modern computer could try every one in less time than it took to transmit the message in the first place.

A better method is required. One way would be to make the encryption not follow any alphabetical sequence.

A B C D E F . . . .
D E F G H I . . . .

In the above example the key is 3, and any letter in plain text can be encoded by reading the corresponding letter in the line below (and decoded by reversing the process). Now suppose the letters on the encoding line were in no particular order. This would give:

A B C D E F . . . .
X L Q T R A . . . .

Since each of 26 letters could be in any of 26 different positions, the number of possibilities works out at 400 million million million million – more than enough to make the code secure against even the most powerful computer. The snag, though, is that someone has to actually remember what order the letters were in, which is close to impossible for ordinary mortals.

One way to overcome this is to use not a number but a word as the key. For example:

A B C D E F G H I J K L M N O P Q R S T U V W X Y Z
S E C U R I T Y A B D F G H J K L M N O P Q V W X Z

Here the word 'security' is the key, and the rest of the alphabet (minus any letters it contains) follows it on the encoding line. This can be just as effective and has the added advantage that, being a proper word, the key is easier to remember.

Unfortunately for the people who design encryption systems, life is not nearly that simple. There is the matter of the frequency of occurrence of letters. In the English language E is the most widely used letter, followed by T, and so on (frequency tables for the entire alphabet do exist). For the code-breaker, this means the most frequently used letter in an encrypted message originally written in English is likely to represent E. If this substitution is made, and the process repeated for other letters in order of frequency, all it then takes is some intelligent guesswork. For example, if the word 'T?E' appears, the full word is most likely to be 'THE'; the codebreaker now knows what letter corresponds to H. Making this substitution also then provides further clues about other words. Fans of detective fiction might remember this was how Sherlock Holmes solved his case in 'The Adventure of the Dancing Men'.

Transposition

To counter this problem another method, known as transposition, was introduced. Here a key word is written horizontally – omitting any repeated letters – and underneath that a number is written to show the alphabetic order of its letters. What happens then is best explained with an example.

```
C O D E
1 4 2 3
```

The key here is the word 'code', and the numbers underneath reflect the order in which its letters occur in the alphabet (C appears first, followed by D and E, and O comes last). From this the message can be encoded as follows:

```
C O D E
1 4 2 3

T H I S
I S H O
W I T W
O R K S
```

The message in plain text is written horizontally, but it is read out vertically, column by column, in the normal numerical sequence of 1, 2, 3, 4. The encoded message (cipher text) is thus:

TIWOIHTKSOWSHSIR

When this is deciphered back into plain text, with appropriate spaces added, the message can be read as

THIS IS HOW IT WORKS

Using transposition, the frequency of the letters gives no clues about the message, as the letters within each word are out of sequence.

From all of the above, we can see that the perfect encryption system should use both substitution and transposition and should have a key with millions of possible combinations. In other words, it should be something like DES – the Data Encryption Standard.

The Data Encryption Standard

DES was developed by IBM in the 1970s and can now be found in a great many commercial products. Its strength comes from the fact that its key is derived mathematically from multiplying two massive prime numbers and then transposing the message several times. After that, only the most powerful computers in the world could hope to decipher it – and even then it would take weeks of work. In fact the American National Security Agency, the equivalent to Britain's GCHQ, is reportedly worried about the strength of this encoding system – although it has to be said other reports suggest the opposite is true. According to the latter, the

NSA is able to defeat the system and is only saying otherwise to fool people into using DES instead of using systems it has yet to break. (With paranoia at that level who knows where the truth is hidden.)

Even so, powerful as DES is, it still has the traditional weakness of all encryption routines: the key. If that is lost, stolen or intercepted, the system falls apart. This is a problem because the key has got to be sent. How else can the recipient decode the message?

RSA

One way is to guard the key very carefully; another is to use a system named after its creators and known as RSA or, more fully, Rivest-Shamir-Adelman.

Every so often an invention appears which seems impossible, which can only be proved with pages full of complex mathematical formulae, and yet which works flawlessly. Into this category falls RSA. Instead of using one key it uses two, a public key and a private key. The clever part is that, whatever key is used to encode the message, it cannot be used to decode it – but the message can be decoded by the other key. And, even if one key is known, there is still no way of using it to generate the second.

In practice this system can be used easily, and that is what counts. To begin with each organization using RSA creates two keys, one public and one private. The public key is distributed widely (literally to anyone who asks), while the private key is kept secure within the organization. Then if two companies – call them A and B – want to communicate, the procedure is simple. Company A encrypts the file using B's public key, knowing that the same key cannot decipher it; only B can do that, by using its private key. A message can thus be safely transmitted and is capable of being read only by its intended recipient. Since no key is ever sent there can be no danger of its being intercepted and decoded by an unauthorized party.

As an added security feature, the message can first be encrypted using the sender's private key and then re-encrypted using the receiver's public key. If the recipient then reverses the process, first by using its private key followed by the sender's public key, the message becomes readable again – and the receiver knows that it must be genuine. No fake message from a different source could ever be deciphered by that exact arrangement of keys, so the identity of the sender is confirmed in a process usually referred to as a digital signature.

Using File Encryption

Fortunately for average users, all this takes place behind the scenes. They have to do no more than use a piece of software much like any other, although they do still have to take care. Like any other security device, though, encryption systems are most vulnerable at the point where human operators become involved. Most often it is their inattention to procedure, or their lack of awareness, that causes disaster. With this in mind, here are some points that should be noted.

Avoid Command Recall Utilities

There are many commercially available software utilities which store the commands that have been entered via the keyboard, so that they can be redisplayed and reused. While these can be very useful – especially for anyone working in DOS – they also mean that a hacker can discover any passwords used simply by pressing the cursor-control keys. The real danger of these utilities is that they work invisibly: nothing warns the user this software is operating. It is even possible for a thief to install such a utility without anyone else even knowing.

This explains another, related point. Avoid encryption software that takes a password on the same command line as the file to be encrypted. Having passwords stolen is one thing, but letting a thief know both the password and the file it refers to is making it just *too* easy.

Do Not Rely on Built-in Solutions

Many applications include their own password-protection system to protect confidential files. These are neither powerful enough nor secure enough to provide anything other than minimal security – and they provide even less if that file is sent over the Internet. Software already exists to defeat most such systems, and it is freely available to anyone who wants it, straight from the Internet.

Do Not Leave Unencrypted Files on the Hard Disk

Once a document has been encrypted, there is still the problem of ensuring the security of the original (unencrypted) file. Just deleting it from the hard drive is far from good enough, as a number of commercially available packages can recover deleted files. Fortunately the same packages that offer file-recovery measures also include programs to permanently erase any file. They should always be used.

Beware the Windows Swap File

A computer can only store so much in its memory. With DOS, Windows and one or more applications all taking up ever increasing amounts of that memory, there is usually very little left over for the document currently being worked on. Windows overcomes this problem by continually swapping sections of the document out of memory and into a specially reserved part of the hard disk known as the swap file. This is a purely temporary arrangement and is part of Windows' normal operating routine; when it is finally saved, the document is actually saved to a different part of the disk. Nonetheless fragments of it will remain in the swap file. As these fragments will be unencrypted, the swap file must be either wiped clean or, if that proves difficult, completely erased. Windows can create another swap file far more easily than the organization can recover from the theft of information.

Be Wary of Names and Titles

There is a technique of data theft known as a chosen plain text attack. If the encryption system is known, an attempt is made to deduce the key by encrypting various phrases likely to be found in the message and comparing them with the original. (An example might be something like 'Bob Jones: Head of Marketing'.) If a match is found anywhere in the text, this reveals the key, which can then be applied to the rest of the message. Despite its apparent simplicity this method has been proved to work on average twenty per cent of the time. For this reason be careful about including names or job titles within encrypted text. They are what the hacker is looking for.

Other Basics

Although the entire subject of encryption is fraught with problems, both legal and political, the general commercial user is unlikely to be affected. For such users more mundane issues should remain a high priority. In practical terms the watchwords are these:

Keep passwords secure. A stolen password is a stolen file.
Use a different password for each file. Letting a thief have access to one file is bad enough, but if the same password

also unlocks other files it could be disastrous.

Be careful with archived material. If a file is archived, someone will still have to remember – or make a note of – the password. Otherwise, how can the file be accessed later?

Do not overuse the encryption system. The more examples thieves have to work with, the higher the chances of their finding the key. Therefore, insist that any messages sent through this highly secure channel be appropriately confidential; as with the allocation of security gradings to documents, the tendency to overclassify should be resisted. (Obviously terms like 'appropriately confidential' are subjective in the extreme and will always vary from company to company. Perhaps the best advice of all, therefore, is to do whatever suits the individual circumstances. Technology can only provide the tools; how they are used is up to the manager.)

Choosing File-encryption Software

Of course, the manager has a further problem to solve of choosing the right tool for the job. How, from the wide range of encryption software available, can he choose the right one? This is more of a problem than it might seem, because any encryption system is only secure until someone breaks it. Any system can be proved to be insecure, but no system can be guaranteed to be safe.

How can anyone without a degree in mathematics or cryptography, or years of practice as a code-breaker, choose a software package on which the entire future of the organization might depend? The first thing to be aware of is the length of the key, which is something the manufacturers usually quote in their advertising. A key 128 bits (digits) long will have many more possible permutations than a 40-bit key, making it that much harder to break, but other factors also need to be considered.

In a world where code-breaking packages can be downloaded from the Internet and run on a standard PC the only safe policy begins and ends with thorough testing. The major point to be tested is the efficiency of the encryption algorithm (an algorithm is the exact sequence of steps a computer program is designed to take to do a particular job). Fortunately, these algorithms – and therefore the encryption package itself – can be tested relatively easily using standard file-compression software. Whereas file-compression software works by searching for repeating patterns of code within the file, encryption packages randomize the file, so there should be no repeating patterns for the compression software to find. Therefore, the better the encryption the less a file can be compressed.

Based on this, the way to test an encryption package is as follows:

Obtain, or create, sample files typical of those that will be encrypted.

Encrypt them.

Compress them.

Compare the length of the encrypted files before and after compression.

It is generally considered that if a file can be compressed by more than five per cent then the encryption is too weak; the data has not been sufficiently randomized, and patterns exist which a code-breaker can use. Anything less than five-per-cent compression means the package is strong enough, and purchasing decisions can be based on more mundane considerations like price or ease of use.

8   Computer Viruses

Of all the subjects that can be grouped together under the heading of Information Technology, there has probably been more rubbish talked about viruses than about all the others put together. Even now there are those who claim that banks take their computers off-line every Friday the Thirteenth because of the risk of virus attack. Needless to say, nothing like that ever happens, and for two very good reasons. Firstly, if the banks had a virus problem it would make more sense to use anti-virus software regularly than to spend a day without computer support. Secondly, if any organization decided not to use its computers on any day when a virus was due to trigger, it would have to leave them permanently switched off. According to a calendar of such events prepared by virus expert Dr Alan Solomon there are a total of 77 viruses likely to become active in January alone (not counting Friday the Thirteenth).

So viruses are apparently both no problem and a major problem – which, paradoxically, describes the situation exactly. Unchecked they can cause a tremendous amount of damage, but they can also be detected and destroyed. In that respect at least they are more of an inconvenience.

It might be a good idea if the issue was put into perspective. At the last count there were over 12,000 known viruses in existence. Of these only about a hundred have ever been found in the outside world (and only ten of those account for most infections). The rest get sent directly to the virus-protection companies by the people who wrote them; usually this is meant as a challenge to see who is the cleverer: the writer of a virus designed to stay hidden or the writer of software designed to find it. However, the companies have no way to be sure that they are the sole recipients. For all they know, the virus they have been sent could also have been released into the wider world. For that reason they have no choice but to act on the assumption that it could appear at any time, and so they announce the discovery of a new virus. This adds to the total of known viruses but does not actually increase the threat of virus attack in the slightest.

Why anybody might want to create a virus is still a matter of debate. According to one legend it all began with a disgruntled programmer working for IBM; according to another it all began behind the Iron Curtain, as an act of hi-tech defiance against the state, which owned all the software. Both could be true, or neither, but in the long run it makes no difference. In practical terms all that really counts is that viruses exist. One particular incident could be of interest, though. A virus-writer known as the Dark Avenger, and perhaps significantly based in Bulgaria, once gave an interview over the Internet. In it he, she or they insisted that virus writers were on the side of the angels, as they punished anyone who used illegally copied software. The logic of this was that, if everyone bought their software from reputable sources, no virus could ever get into their system. Self-justifying as that sounds, it does have to be said that the more dubious the source of software, the more likelihood there is of an infection – and this is something it would be well to remember.

What is a Virus?

According to most textbooks it is 'a piece of self-replicating code' – which only makes sense to people who know enough about computers to write the textbooks, but is meaningless to anyone else. This is unfortunate because it is precisely those without such learning who need the help. And yet a virus can be explained easily, if somewhat simplistically.

First, consider the COPY command built into the instruction set of each computer: the routine that takes a named file and copies it to another disk or to another part of the same disk. Now suppose that, instead of the user issuing this command, another program issued it automatically whenever a certain event occurred – for example, on a particular date. If the command and the program were then connected together and the file named to be copied was the program itself, the result would be a self-replicating program, better known as a virus (a very primitive form of virus obviously, but a virus nevertheless). The only differences are that this proto-virus stays in plain view, while the real thing hides itself inside any other program it can find, and that a real virus also carries a payload: a third program, which comes into operation whenever some predefined condition is satisfied.

This may do nothing more than show a stupid message on your screen, like 'Your computer is now stoned. Legalize Marijuana' (the Stoned virus). There are others like the Cascade virus, the media's favourite, which causes all letters to fall to the bottom of the screen. Then there are those that become active on the anniversary of anything from the Gulf War to the Tiananmen Square massacre to remind everyone of what happened, and usually add an opinion or two. These do no damage in themselves and can usually be cleared either by pressing the escape (Esc) key or by pressing the CTRL, ALT and Delete keys simultaneously although as this second method re-boots (re-starts) the computer any unsaved work will be lost. In some cases the computer has to be physically switched off, again with the loss of any unsaved work, but the computer will at least work properly when switched back on. After that no one will know the virus is there – until the next time it attacks.

However, anyone who lets a situation like that continue is risking more than just the loss of any unsaved work. If computer files are sent outside the company and are subsequently found to contain a virus, even if only one of the harmless variety, then that company's reputation as a reliable trading partner will suffer immeasurably. This is because the people who received those files, and found the virus, will know even a harmless virus is a clear sign that the company where the virus came from has no secure policy to stop them spreading – and where there are harmless viruses a malicious virus can also lurk.

That being the case the best advice for anyone who finds a virus attacking their computer is to do nothing until someone competent has been called for. Even if the virus can be cleared easily leave it there both as proof that it exists and, much more importantly, because it is not always easy to tell when a virus is malicious or harmless. Only then can the safe procedure be followed as explained later.

Always remember there are some viruses which can do real damage. If a system is infected with one of these malicious viruses all the data on an entire computer network could be destroyed – and it could happen in less time than in takes to read this sentence.

All of a sudden the threat can be seen. It might not be as omnipresent as the media suggests, but when it hits, it hits hard. For that reason alone, every step must be taken to keep viruses well away from computers. The whole of Western civilization is not about to collapse, but the same cannot necessarily be said about a company that is already trading under difficult economic conditions.

To make matters worse, not everything that attacks a computer is a virus. Other entities can do just as much damage, although they are not defined as viruses. These are logic bombs, Trojan horses and Worms.

Logic Bombs

These are small additions to much larger programs, usually (but not always) added by the original programmer. As the name implies, these can be devastating when something triggers them off – and that event would typically be removing a particular name from the payroll.

Logic bombs are aimed at a specific target, like an ex-employer. They offer no threat to any other system, nor even to any other computer, but being tailored to do a particular job means they can inflict far more damage than a virus ever could. They are also virtually undetectable, so there is only one line of defence against them: regular data backups.

Trojan Horses

Like the original Trojan horse, this is one thing concealed within another. The 'horse' is a piece of apparently harmless software, like a game, but once that starts running the 'Trojan' element appears. A second program, hidden in the first, goes into action and either immediately destroys all the data held on that computer, or else leaves a destructive program that will do the job several hours later. Usually the time delay option is favoured, so that no one can make the connection between the software and the data loss.

This is a particularly malicious piece of software. No anti-virus package can detect it, nor does it need to stay hidden. Once again, the best, if not the only, defence is regular data backups.

Worms

As they originated in a mainframe environment Worms can lay claim to having been the first viruses. Everything else came after them – including even the payload, which they lack. Instead they work against mainframe computers, or networks, by jamming the communication system. This they do by multiplying across the data links (cables) until no other, legitimate, message can get through. At that point the system collapses, choked into submission.

Only a virus is 'infectious' and can spread from file to file or from disk to disk. A virus on a hard disk can copy itself on to a floppy, from which in turn it can copy itself on to another hard disk – spreading the virus and, more importantly, spreading the payload. That is where the danger comes from. A single virus can not only attack a single computer, it can find its way on to every computer in the organization. Remember, too, that, even if their intention is just to create a stupid message, viruses can still do a lot of damage inadvertently. They are not particularly well written and, given the circumstances of their creation, they are unlikely to be thoroughly tested. Therefore, anti-virus software is highly recommended.

Anti-virus Software

Perhaps by now it will come as no surprise that this particular type of software can work in a number of ways. As ever in the computer industry one problem produces many solutions – in this case three: signature-scanning, file checksumming and activity monitoring.

Although Worms are self-replicating and therefore a virus by definition they are considered separately here because they do not hide themselves inside, i.e. infect, other files. For the rest of this chapter, then, assume a virus to be as that originally described (although be assured anti-virus software can also detect Worms).

Signature-scanning

As each virus is in some way different, it follows that each will have a small section of programming code which is unique (its signature). Signature-scanning works by searching for this in every file capable of holding a virus, and checking each file against a database of all known signatures.

Simple as that might sound, there are problems involved. Not the least of these is the sheer length of time it can take to check every possible file against the signature of all known viruses. On any reasonably sized system that can be enough to test the patience of any computer-user. This, of course, introduces the risk that no one will use the software, because no one can spare the time. To avoid this, many products include a 'quick-scan' option which searches for the hundred or so viruses which are known to exist in the outside world. This is obviously quicker, but it does carry with it the risk that a virus not thought to be 'in the wild' (the outside world) could remain undetected – until it strikes.

A further problem is that this database of known signatures must be regularly updated with new additions. By itself this is very little trouble, except it takes time to install the update on every machine, and it costs money to keep up the subscription charges for the service.

There might be those who think that, if only a small number of viruses is likely to appear on their computers, a basic package without upgrades is all they need. Unfortunately, tempting as it might sound, this would be a very big mistake. Not only would new viruses remain undetected, but known viruses appearing in the wild for the first time would also slip through the net. And this is on top of any problems caused by a thing known as polymorphism.

In the continuous technological arms race between virus author and virus detector, polymorphism is the latest weapon. Basically the versatile nature of the computer microchip means there is more than one way of doing the same job – which, in this context, means the virus's signature can be changed, and it becomes polymorphic. In fact it is now possible for the signature to be changed every single time the virus copies itself, which makes it virtually undetectable by standard scanners. Furthermore, in what has to be the height of irresponsibility, so-called polymorphism engines – software which can change any virus into a polymorph – are now freely available over the Internet.

There is a defence against this. Scanners now check both for signatures and also for the unique piece of code which signifies polymorphism. This development, if it does nothing else, at least shows the importance of keeping anti-virus software up to date. Anything less means the company could be facing the technological equivalent of laser-guided 'smart' bombs armed only with a bow and arrow.

File Checksumming

In principle this can be explained easily. Since a virus hides itself inside other files, the length of the host file must be increased, because it now contains extra lines of code. Therefore, if a file suddenly grows, the chances are a virus is at work.

When it is first installed, a file checksummer creates a 'magic number' for its file, based on its length and other factors (which are kept secret, for obvious reasons). This number is then stored, and encrypted in some cases, so that it can be used as a check against future calculations. Thereafter, whenever the program is run the magic number for each file is recalculated and compared against the original. If it matches, the file is clean, but if there are any differences the alarm is raised.

On the face of it, this is a quick, easy, almost foolproof method. Yet even this has its problems. Firstly, there are many legitimate reasons why a file might change. Setup information, like the colour of the background screen or the size of the characters being displayed, are all stored in the file, so any changes to the setup changes the file. At this point the question of 'crying wolf' raises its head, because too many false alarms can lead to complacency. Worse still, the alarms can be ignored or given such a low priority that a virus has time to strike before the file is disinfected (cleaned). Needless to say such day to day activity as adding data to file, or deleting data from it, will have no effect as these do not change the way the computer operates.

Finally, quick and easy as file checksumming is, it still has one basic flaw: when it is installed the file must be free of viruses. If the computer is already infected, the length of both file and virus will be incorporated into the magic number, making the system totally ineffective. To solve this a signature scanner must first be used.

Activity Monitoring

This guards against the actual activities of a virus by monitoring all computer operations, and alerts the user when 'unreasonable' activity is noticed. However, no one has yet adequately defined what constitutes reasonable or unreasonable behaviour. As with file checksumming, a change could be made for legitimate reasons, or it could be caused by a virus, and so the danger of false alarms is just as great.

Policy Guidelines

In practice anti-virus software is only half the story. Like any other form of security, it needs an effective policy alongside it. A code of practice should therefore be established which everyone must follow, without exception. This should include the following precautions.

Check all Disks on a Dedicated Machine

Before any floppy disk is allowed into the system it should first be checked for viruses on a computer dedicated exclusively to this job. Within the industry this is known as a 'sheep dip'.

Suitably prepared, any potentially obsolete computer can be used. First, format the hard disk – which is guaranteed to remove all viruses – then install the anti-virus software. After that use it for no other purpose than virus checking. (Naturally, it should also be disconnected from any networks.) There will then be at least one clean machine to act as a barrier between the main computer system and any source of infection.

Be Careful of Compressed Files

It is now virtually standard practice for companies to compress their software before transferring it to floppy disk. Briefly, this involves searching each file for recurring patterns of binary code and replacing them with a much smaller token. When the files are decompressed back to full size, this token is automatically replaced with the correct piece of code. Systems such as these can almost double the space available on a floppy disk, but from a security point of view they have one major drawback: by removing fragments of code they mask the virus signatures.

The correct procedure is to scan all disks with the files still in their compressed state (a virus might be hidden in the decompression program which could infect the sheep dip machine). Then decompress all files to a hard disk and scan them again. Only if that second scan reveals nothing can they be allowed on to the main system.

Some software packages claim to be able to scan for viruses even in compressed files, but this option should be ignored. What with new viruses and polymorphic versions of old viruses, the job is hard enough to begin with; why make it harder? As scanning compressed files saves so very little time, doing it trades a major risk for a minor advantage.

Forbid all Unauthorized Software

Software can be virus-free and yet still represent a threat to the organization, as in the case of a Trojan horse. Because of this, the only safe policy is to forbid the use of all unauthorized software. Conventionally, this is usually taken to mean a general ban on computer games – the supposed source of all infections – but in practice the ban must be far more wide ranging.

Any disk, no matter how supposedly reputable the source, must not be allowed anywhere near the main computer system until its use has been authorized. The incident of the so-called AIDS virus should serve as a warning to all. This involved disks that were apparently sent to companies from a government organization claiming to give employers all the information they needed to protect their employees from the threat of AIDS. These employers then ran the software only to find their computers suddenly paralysed, with a screen message telling them how much it would cost to get their data back. Exactly how much the extortionists made from this will never be known, because no company was prepared to admit that it had been so careless – and even when the police caught the two people responsible, no one would press charges.

Be warned. No matter where the disk supposedly comes from, always check the return address is real and not fictitious, and *never* run it on a machine holding valuable data. Not every disk is a threat, but it makes good sense to act as if it were.

Disks Taken Home Must be Checked

From time to time everyone takes work home, and they probably always will. In terms of comfort and convenience there is no better way of working – and also no better way of contracting a virus.

That home computer is very likely used by all the family, which means software will come from every source imaginable, including disks swapped in the school playground. So, if work must be brought into the office on a disk, check it thoroughly.

Not Every Problem is a Virus

If a computer starts behaving erratically, a virus is only one of a list of possible causes. It could be a bug in the software. This can be checked by following exactly the same procedure on another computer. If the same problem occurs, a bug is more likely than a virus, and the software manufacturer should be contacted. Very likely they will know about this and have a fix already prepared. Also remember the problem could be caused by a logic bomb or Trojan horse.

Educate Staff

The best defence against any virus is staff who know what has to be done and why. If a formal training course is more than the budget allows, then at the very least the IT Manager or Departmental head should talk to the staff stressing the importance of virus protection.

Be Wary of Downloads

Any file downloaded from the Internet, Bulletin Boards or just received through E-mail should be thoroughly checked before being used. Of particular importance here is the threat from the so-called Macro viruses, which attach themselves to wordprocessor and spreadsheet files. Macros are nothing more than tiny programs designed to automate certain repetitive functions within a particular spreadsheet or wordprocessor, so they are for the most part legitimate. There are very many good reasons why a macro would be attached to such a document. However, some can do as much damage as any other virus, so care must be taken.

Unless the source of the document can be absolutely guaranteed, always open it with the Macro Autorun feature disabled. It is also a good idea to check the Macro listing, specifically looking for the AutoSave and AutoOpen commands which are invariably found as part of the virus (they are needed to help it spread to other files). Needless to say, the best idea of all is to invest in anti-virus software capable of spotting these Macro viruses before the file is opened.

Use Anti-virus Software Regularly

Anti-virus software should also be used regularly. The recommended practice is to use two different products: one installed permanently on each computer; the other kept by the IT Department or a named individual. One can be cynical, and point out that the people recommending two packages are the same people who earn a living by selling them, but in this case their voice should be heard. Even the best software can fail to detect a particular virus, but the second package should always spot it. Furthermore, some viruses will load themselves into computer memory when the machine is switched on and so become almost undetectable. By running a second package from a floppy disk with the system start-up files included (i.e. a system disk) the normal hard-disk routines are avoided, preventing the virus from loading and making it detectable.

Even so, between all the scans and despite all the checks, a virus could still get through. Should this actually happen the first (and second) rule is, don't panic. If possible close any files and quit any applications to make data recovery easier then switch off the computer. After that, the hard work really begins.

Quarantine the affected computer.
Isolate all the disks associated with it.
Check every other computer.
Check every single disk.

From all this it becomes readily apparent that removing a virus is far harder than preventing it from getting there in the first place. What better incentive could there be for implementing a secure anti-virus policy.

9 E-mail, Bulletin Boards and the Internet

In the minds of most people (and all of the media) these terms are interchangeable, whereas in fact they are entirely separate creations. Each serves a different function; each operates in a different way; and each has its own security problems. True, they all involve sending data from one computer to another, but after that all similarity ends. The Internet spans the entire world, while with E-mail the data sent might not even leave the office.

As much as anything else, the confusion is caused by the fact that one can often provide a service to another: for example, E-mail can be sent over the Internet. In this respect at least they are close enough to be considered as a single entity; nevertheless, there are differences, and those differences are important. Some security measures can apply equally to all three, but there are times when each needs special consideration. First, though, they should each be explained.

E-mail

E (for Electronic)-mail is a rarity in the computer world in having a name that describes it exactly. As with traditional mail, a letter is sent from one address to the other; the only difference is that with E-mail the letter is sent electronically, and the address is another computer.

The computer which accepts this incoming mail, and obviously transmits it as well, is known as the post office and should only accept mail from recognized callers (who are usually referred to as a remote user). If this is not possible – in a system open to the public for example – at the very least a remote user's account should be established at the post office, to separate external mail from the corporate internal mail. Different telephone lines are also a good idea.

On the subject of good ideas, the myth of the so-called 'Good Times' virus should be laid to rest. According to popular mythology this is an E-mail message with the heading 'GOOD TIMES' which, when received, proceeds to format the hard drive and destroy everything on it in the process. This does not exist.

If anyone is nevertheless still worried by it, or by any other possible method of formatting the hard drive by remote control, protection is simple. Simply remove a file called ANSI.SYS, which can be found in CONFIG.SYS. Remote commands need this to do their dirty work. Alternatively, if ANSI.SYS is needed for a piece of legitimate software, make sure the version of DOS being used is 3.3 or above, and label the hard disk (using the DOS command LABEL). From that moment on, whenever the command FORMAT C: is issued, the computer will ignore it unless the correct label is also specified.

Anyone still worried or who has ever received a message similar to the Good Times hoax, and there are plenty in circulation, should turn to the Internet and check out the various web sites which exist to counter these wild claims. A good place to start would be the sites of suppliers of anti-virus software, followed by *www av.ibm.com* and also *www.kumite.com/myths*. There are others, too, so anyone seriously worried should have no problem in finding someone capable of putting their mind at rest.

Bulletin Boards

This is the electronic equivalent of the notice-board. Notices are pinned to it for anyone to read, and anyone can pin notices to it. Simply dial up the number, get past the welcome screen, and the system is there to be used (or abused).

In the mythology of computerdom, bulletin boards are beaten only by computer games as a way of letting a virus into the organization. It is true viruses have been found there (and checking every file is still a wise precaution), but in reality they are far less than the hype suggests. The Systems Operators (Sysops) who run these bulletin boards are, by definition, highly computer-literate and well aware of the virus problem and of the precautions they must take to counter the threat. On a commercially operated bulletin board their jobs depend on it.

A far greater problem is the risk run by companies who operate their own bulletin boards – to keep their sales team informed, for example. Unless precautions are taken, hackers can use these as an entry into the system proper.

The Internet

During the Cold War, American scientists became worried about maintaining communications between various defence and research establishments in the event of a nuclear attack. Work on the problem led to a system in which each computer would intelligently route its calls through whatever telephone exchanges were available. If one was out of action the computer would, instead, send its message to another computer somewhere else, which would take the call and automatically send it through a different exchange. In this way, no matter how much of the country was devastated, the message would always get through.

From such beginnings grew the Internet as it is today: a gigantic linked system of databases and discussion groups, there to be used by anyone for the price of a local phone call. Throughout the world gateways exist, connecting every user to whatever service they need entirely free; all they pay for is the phone call to the gateway and a monthly subscription to the Internet Service Provider (ISP).

The Internet is, therefore, owned by no one, controlled by no one, beyond the reach of governments – and a security nightmare.

To recap: E-mail can be sent directly from one computer to another, with the first computer simply dialling the telephone number of the second. This is *not* the Internet. However, if the two computers are some distance apart it could be cheaper for them both to make use of the Internet, paying for two local phone calls instead of one long-distance call; for time-consuming calls that are made regularly, the cost saving could be considerable. Alternatively, if the same information has to be sent to a lot of people, it might be more cost-effective to set up a company bulletin board and post the information to that. This also is not the Internet. But another option could be to set up a bulletin board that is part of the Internet – i.e. a Web site – to reduce costs.

Pedantic as all this seems, it is important, because each method has its own particular security risks, and each calls for different security measures.

Security Measures

E-mail

Even if E-mail messages are sent directly, and not via the Internet, there are still security issues to consider – although of a limited nature. During transmission the only possible threat is wire-tapping, which can be ignored for most practical purposes. Companies would have to be sending very sensitive data indeed before that became a viable option for a thief. Much more likely is that a thief will read the message once it has been received.

E-mail messages are not necessarily read immediately; like messages sent by the traditional post, they could wait for hours (even days) before being looked at. In companies operating across different time zones this would be guaranteed to happen. Yet the messages would still be on the receiving computers' hard disks, where they could be read by anyone.

To guard against this some E-mail packages protect their messages behind a password protection system so only those who know the password are allowed to read the mail. Others use Receipt Notification. To explain: whenever an E-mail message arrives, a symbol appears on the screen of the receiving computer to announce the fact. The message can be read immediately or left until later; either way, the moment someone presses the button to start reading the message, its sender is automatically notified of the fact, together with the time it happened. If that time is outside normal working hours questions should be asked. The reader might just be someone working late – or it might be an intruder.

Receipt Notification might not be the most secure method, but sometimes nothing else is available. Most proprietary E-mail packages routinely encrypt every message sent, but this only works if both sender and recipient are using the same software. If they are using different packages the only option is to use plain text. The alternative is to standardize on one type of software – a solution that is easy to implement for mail within the organization, but a lot harder for messages going outside.

The Internet

Weak as it seems, Receipt Notification is the Ban
compared to the Internet. There everything

123

system known as Transport Control Protocol/Internet Protocol or TCP/IP for short. (Anyone involved with electronic communications is likely to find this particular set of initials appearing regularly, because it is this protocol which allows a computer running under one system to communicate with another running an entirely different system.) The basis for the Internet it might be, but it does have one serious drawback: it allows data sent over the Internet to be read by anyone, whether authorized or not.

A recent, and unfortunately true, story highlights the extent of the problem. In central Florida Internet users were denied access to the system for several days, not because of hardware failure but because of action taken by the Internet Service Provider. During the course of a security check the provider found several of its machines were running so-called sniffer programs, which spy on information going out over the Internet and are used to capture log-in procedures and passwords. So serious was the problem that the provider had to take the drastic (yet widely praised) action of replacing all passwords that gave access rights to its system – leaving subscribers effectively locked out until they could be notified of the changes.

Anyone who believes that this story belongs in the 'only in America' category should think again. It could have happened anywhere in the world. It could even be happening somewhere else right now. This is why there are two cardinal rules for send-

k of England
s handled by a

encryption software, so that it
but the authorized reader.
security procedures must be
s like sniffer programs. Also,
be stored on its computers
this data should be kept

Bulletin Boards

As for bulletin boards, they present a range of problems all their own. Some are associated only with the Internet, but others would still have to be faced even if the Internet ceased to exist. For the sake of logical progression bulletin boards will be dealt with first, leaving web sites until later.

Never Reveal Passwords over the Telephone

The easiest way for a hacker to get the access password is to ring up and ask for it (known in the trade as social engineering). Simple that may be, but it also happens to be highly effective. One trick is to ring up an inexperienced, or untrained, computer operator claiming to be the police who are monitoring a thief right at that moment and who only need the log-in password to catch him in the act. Alternatively the caller could claim to be someone from another office who has forgotten the password, to be from a software company hired to test the system, or any one of a thousand variations. Every single story will sound reasonable, but all will be bogus.

Needless to say, the police will never need a password, nor will software companies, British Telecom or anyone else. In every case it will be a thief, and staff should be made aware of this. No matter how persuasive, threatening, abusive or belligerent callers may be, under no circumstances should they be given any passwords.

Be Careful about Welcome Screens

Legal experts are reportedly worried over the forms of words which appear on most bulletin boards' welcome screens. Usually they take the form of the company name followed by a courteously phrased invitation to enter the password. On the surface that seems quite straightforward, but apparently it is not. The lawyers point out that any request to enter the password would

125

make it very difficult for a company later to argue that access was unauthorized. (How could it be? The hacker was invited.) Such a view has yet to be tested in the courts, but most legal experts agree that this will only be a matter of time. The law is too vague, and the loophole too tempting.

Anyone not wanting to make legal history by being involved in a test case should therefore think strongly about changing the welcome screen on their bulletin board. First, remove the company name; authorized users already know it, so leaving it in place just helps the hackers (they know whose switchboard to call so they can ask for the passwords). Secondly, change the wording of the log-in request to something like: 'This system is for authorized users only. Any unauthorized use will result in prosecution under the 1990 Computer Misuse Act.' Users should also be asked to enter 'yes' or 'no' to indicate that they accept these conditions. If the answer is 'no', the system should shut down immediately.

The new screen may be a lot less friendly than the old, but it is also much more secure.

Set Time Limits
Some bulletin boards are only needed during office hours. If so, shut them down at night and leave them switched off at weekends. The less time they operate for, the less time a hacker has to penetrate the system.

Set the Modem to wait for Several Rings
There is a thing called a demon dialler attack, in which a computer automatically tries every telephone number in an area and logs those answered by a modem for later investigation. Setting the modem to answer only after several rings means that, by the time it does answer, the thief computer will have already rung off. This keeps the network hidden from potential hackers.

Specify Read and Write Access

If users need only to *take* information from the bulletin board – for example, if they are salesmen wanting the latest price information – then the system should be specified as read-only. If no one can write to the computer hard disk, no one can leave a virus on it.

In the same way, anyone who only needs to enter information into the system has no reason to read any files. They should not be given the chance, so the system should be specified as write-only.

Consider Using Dial-back Facilities

Some software packages offer a dial-back facility: once a user dials in, the software hangs up the line and then immediately calls back the number associated with that particular user. In this way, even if a thief discovers a password, it will do no more than generate a phone call to a legitimate user – which, if it is not expected, should be taken as an alarm message.

This prevents hackers breaking into the system, but it does have the drawback in that each user is restricted to a single telephone number. A travelling executive calling from a number other than the one associated with him would be denied access, and this could make the system unsuitable for some organizations.

Remote Access

Closely allied to bulletin boards is a system known as remote access, which allows personnel who are away from base to log into the system over a telephone line and use the computer on their own desk as if they were inside the same building and physically connected to the corporate network. With the rise of tele-working (employees working at home, rather than at the office), this is becoming increasingly popular – although, needless to say, the security implications are tremendous. Steps have to be taken

COMPUTER SECURITY: BUSINESSES AT RISK ·

to protect the corporate data, beginning with the measures outlined above (what works for bulletin boards also works for remote access). After that:

Restrict directory access. The office computer holding the remote-access software must be protected, which at the very least means restricting access to the directories concerned. If the access software includes its own password protection, use that as well. Then no one can secretly change the log-in passwords or call-back numbers.

Enable drive security. Callers do not necessarily need access to the entire system, so keep them out of sensitive areas.

Use encryption options. If the software includes an encryption option, always use it. The protection it offers might be weak, but it will deter the casual hacker.

Restrict keyboard entry. Most software has what is known as a chat mode which allows a two-way conversation between a remote user calling in from outside and a local user inside the office (although obviously the conversation is text on a screen and not the spoken word). The danger here is that a local user inside the office could be asked for the password to a restricted section of the computer system and will have even less reason to be suspicious than if the request was made over the telephone. Perhaps it goes without saying, but passwords should still not be given out. That remote user is more likely to be a hacker.

If a connection is lost, restart the computer. A lost connection is more often than not caused by some form of illegal activity, so make life difficult for the hacker by configuring the software to restart (reboot) the computer every time it happens.

There might be some companies regularly receiving legitimate calls over an unreliable telephone line who would find this constant re-booting of their computers too expen-

128

sive in terms of lost productivity. If so, a balance will have to be found between protection and productivity; something that can only be done on an individual basis.

Set inactivity time-outs. If no one is using the remote computer, disconnect it. Not only will this save the phone bill, it will also prevent unattended computers being used for illegal purposes.

Regularly check audit logs. Find out who has been using the system and how often. Apart from checking the obvious points (such as users accessing parts of the system for which they have no authorization), look out for browse attacks. These happen when a hacker first penetrates system security; typically, the hacker checks out the directories on offer and then logs off, returning later when the directories have been studied and the most promising selected for further exploration. If an audit log shows that someone did nothing more than list directories, a hacker has been at work, and security measures should be radically upgraded as a matter of priority.

Security can be increased by careful naming of the directories. A directory or sub-directory called \PASSWDS\ would be a prime target, but if the name was changed to something less revealing, the hacker would have no idea what was inside it. Unfortunately, changing directory names on an already installed network would be far from easy, if it were even possible. In any new installation, though, it would be a good idea not to accept the manufacturer's ease-of-use names; instead, when the opportunity of choosing directory names is offered, choose something different.

Another trick is to create several dummy directories, complete with sub-directories (and perhaps even sub-sub-directories) of their own, giving them inviting-sounding names. The more directories a hacker has to choose from, the less chance there is of an important directory being found. To be more precise, those important directories will be found, but it will take longer – which increases the likelihood of detection. Just as importantly, if the audit log ever shows someone accessing those blank, dummy, directories it would be clear proof that a hacker had been at work (who else would go near them?). In this way a great deal of extra security can be traded for a minimal amount of disk space.

Keep the monitor away from general view. If the monitor attached to the office computer can be seen by everyone during remote-access sessions, onlookers could acquire information that would be invaluable if they wanted to use the system illegally. There are those who suggest the screen should be blanked, but this obviously makes it difficult to provide any kind of technical support, and could in itself mask unauthorized use. Just keeping the monitor away from the curious could be a viable compromise.

Firewalls

The real danger of bulletin boards and remote access – and the reason for most of the security measures associated with them – is that they can allow access to the entire corporate network. Once hackers get past the welcome screen (which offers only a fragile defence at the best of times), they could be free to steal data, corrupt files, leave viruses, or do all three. On a system that is connected to the Internet, with all its millions of users, those dangers are magnified. Against a background like that, extra security measures are strongly recommended for any bulletin boards – and they should be just about mandatory for Internet connections.

Fortunately the technology exists to provide these extra security measures. It takes the generic name of a firewall. The term is generic because some firewalls consist of software only, while others require extra hardware, which makes an exact definition difficult. The situation is not helped by the manufacturers themselves, who use a variety of different expressions to mean exactly the same thing. That said, they do at least all agree that a firewall restricts access to and from the Internet as a means of preventing hacker attacks and other security breaches.

Roughly speaking there are three types of firewall:

Packet filters
Proxy servers/Application firewall
Bastion/Isolation/Host

Packet Filters

All data travelling across the Internet is split into small units, called packets, each also carrying an extra piece of code holding the network address of the computer which sent it. A packet filter simply reads this address and compares it against a predefined list. Those that are 'safe', like an associate company or a branch office, it lets through. All others are barred from the system.

Consisting of software only, this method is cheap and relatively easy to implement. It can be beaten, though. There is a technique known as spoofing, which basically means putting a false address on a packet of data, and so tricking the firewall into believing the data comes from a safe source.

Proxy Servers

This is a combined hardware and software approach. The hardware is a dedicated computer through which passes all traffic to and from the Internet, and the software installed on it subjects the traffic to a much more rigorous examination. As an added bonus this also concentrates all Internet access into one channel, so there is only one point of attack, and hence only one place that needs defending.

Because this examination requires an understanding of the application which first created the data, the technique is also referred to as an application firewall. Its drawback is that every application allowed has to be configured separately.

Bastions

This combines both the types and uses them together. All data passes through both. Alternatively, some of it can pass through packet-filtering only. In this way the low-risk part of the network can be protected by packet-filtering, for minimum delay, while the high-risk part of the network can use both packet-filtering and proxy servers, for maximum security.

If this system is used, care must be taken that the two firewalls operate independently. Just because a packet filter has let data through, that does not mean the proxy server should check it any less thoroughly (packet filters can be spoofed.) Also, if one firewall is beaten, it should offer the hacker no clues as to how to defeat the other. As this method isolates the computer system from the Internet it is also described as an isolation firewall. Similarly as it needs to be closely integrated with the computer operating system it could be said that the firewall is a resident on that system which naturally makes the system itself the host. From this comes the term host firewall.

Stand-alones

For the sake of completeness, it should be added that there is another form of security known as stand-alone. As the name implies, this is a computer that is attached to the Internet but *not* to the office network. With no connection between the two there can be no risk. However, data can only be transferred from one to the other by means of floppy disks, which could get tedious.

Despite all the foregoing, firewalls are only part of the story, and they must be complemented by an adequate security policy.

Internet Security

Before such a policy can be defined, we first need to consider the unique threats that are posed by the Internet. These are:

Unauthorized access.
Disclosure of confidential information.
Virus infection.
Data loss or alteration.
Rogue E-mail.
Staff downloading objectionable material.
Unofficial net surfing.

Some of these are self-explanatory, but others are not quite so obvious. For example, rogue E-mail is the threat posed to a company's business (and reputation) by its staff sending from a company address messages which the company would most definitely not approve of. These could be illegal, insulting or just tasteless, but in all cases the company would suffer.

As to staff downloading objectionable material from the Internet, the law makes no distinction between a picture on a wall and a picture on a computer screen. The sort of images sometimes described as 'glamour', or worse, could therefore leave the company open to a charge of sexual harassment.

It is also most important to remember that, if a computer holds information on private individuals, then the disclosure, loss or alteration of that information is an offence against the Data

Protection Act, for which the company could be prosecuted. (Failure to protect such information is in itself a crime.)

By now it must be obvious that the Internet can be a dangerous place to do business. However, it is also most definitely a place where business can be done, or increased – and this means that businesses have to use it, whatever its dangers.

Anyone considering using the Internet should therefore take the following steps:

Identify the business need.
Assess the risks.
Develop a security policy.
Implement appropriate controls.
Disable inappropriate services.
Monitor and maintain effective security controls.

Identify the business need

Without a clearly defined business need it becomes impossible to decide which services should be bought from the Internet Service Provider (just E-mail, use of the Internet or possession of corporate web site). This means the services being bought could cost more than is necessary and expose the company to greater security threats. There are many reasons why an organization should have an Internet account, but doing it just because the Internet is there is not one of them. At the very least anyone proposing to go online should be able to answer questions such as:

What services are needed?
What will they be used for?
What services will be prohibited?
Who will be responsible for the service?
Who will carry out a risk assessment or produce a security
    policy?

If a page is to be prepared for the World Wide Web (WWW) what information will be published?

If anyone is vague about the answers, or struggles to understand the questions, take that as a sign that the issue has not been sufficiently thought through.

Assess the Risks

To appreciate the threat to which the company is exposed, consider:

The value of the information.
The potential harm resulting from a security breach.
The likelihood of a security breach occurring.

The value of the information is traditionally defined as the value of the corporate data which would be at risk should a hacker penetrate the system via the Internet. In much the same way any potential harm resulting from a security breach is how much it would cost the company should its data be lost, given to a competitor or made public. The likelihood of a security breach occurring is self-explanatory.

Given that the Internet is an inherently insecure system, that no one can control the route any message takes on it, and that it is populated by people who genuinely enjoy intercepting messages, be immediately suspicious of anyone who claims there is no risk at all. Remember also that the Internet Service Provider is not responsible for the security of any information. The more reputable companies will have their own security procedures (and this should be considered when deciding which service to choose), but the ultimate responsibility belongs to the company that owns the information.

135

Develop a Security Policy

In practical terms converting a security policy into a workable set of rules should begin by answering such questions as:

Should all incoming E-mail be allowed, or just that coming from known sites?

Should outgoing E-mail be allowed to any destination, or should it be restricted to specific addresses?

Should data be transferred anywhere, or just to specific sites?

Should data be received from anywhere, or just from specific sites?

Should total access to the World Wide Web (WWW) be allowed, or should it be restricted to specific sites?

From this a workable set of guidelines can be formulated, which can then be made formal by converting them into the security policy itself. This is a statement covering both the connection to and use of the Internet. It should include:

The services that can be used.

Who authorizes connections.

Who is responsible for security.

What standards, guidelines and practices should be followed.

Users' responsibilities.

A copy of the policy should then be given to all staff, not just those who are expected to use the system. (In the fullness of time everyone will become involved, so make sure they all understand the ground rules right from the beginning.) It is also recommended that this policy document be enshrined in the company disciplinary procedures, so that any transgression could potentially lead to dismissal. That might at first appear harsh, but it is not, because the entire company could be at stake. For that reason everyone who receives a copy of the security policy should be made to sign a declaration agreeing to abide by the rules and to accept their punishment if they break them. That way there can be no danger of unfair dismissal charges (although in high-security environments, where the threat might have to be enforced, a lawyer should be consulted over the exact wording used).

Implement Appropriate Controls

Here the key word is 'appropriate'. For some companies that might mean firewalls, for others data encryption or software to prevent a virus being downloaded. This can only be decided on an individual basis. Even so, no matter how slight the apparent risk seems, a measure of staff training must be included. Being aware of the dangers is the first step to avoiding them.

Disable Inappropriate Services

All Internet connection software comes with a wide range of services and options, some of which will be needed, others not. Decide which is which, and do whatever it takes to prevent access to those unneeded services. Having extra facilities on hand should the need arise might seem like a good idea, but it also means they will soon be used by all members of staff, no matter what the risk, cost or time taken. Even worse, they could be the means by which outsiders gain access to the system. At times like this the right course of action can best be described as enlightened paranoia. Assume risk is everywhere, and prohibit everything unless its use can be conclusively justified.

Monitor and Maintain Effective Security Controls

Any unauthorized changes, particularly to firewalls, should be detected immediately and corrected just as fast. Also keep in mind that, as the business changes and the use of the Internet becomes more widespread, the business needs for using it will also change. Before this happens the above procedure should be repeated.

Web Security

As more and more companies set up their own web sites, so the security issues surrounding these should be considered. For the owners of a web site that means regular inspection, to make sure it has not been altered. (If it can happen to the CIA – and it did – it can happen to any web site.) Points to look out for include confirming that the links still point to the right pages and do not take potential customers to a pornographic site or, even worse, that of a competitor. Also, if the site is used for advertising, check that the prices quoted have not been altered, that any telephone numbers are correct, and that no stupid spelling mistakes have been deliberately added. (The last point might seem a trivial one, but nothing makes a site look more unprofessional – and if the web site appears unprofessional, what does that say about the company that owns it?)

Here a good idea is to configure the Browser so it shows the company web site whenever an Internet connection is made. That way a site inspection can take place practically every day.

After that come the problems not of owning a web site but of visiting others which all companies connected to the Internet will do from time to time. Whether it be to find out what competitors are doing on their web sites, for the purposes of market research or for any of the other benefits claimed for Internet access, it can be taken for granted that as soon as a company acquires its own Internet connection other web sites will be visited. Curiosity alone will see to that. Unfortunately, in this case, curiosity can be dangerous and all because of something known as Active Content.

Active Content

Also known as Executable Content, this is the name given to the system which creates the animated graphics which are now appearing on an increasing number of web sites. First to come was a programming language known as Java, closely followed by a Microsoft product known as ActiveX. Both have the same basic flaw: they work by placing executable files directly on to the hard drive. Nowhere on any web browser will there be a warning that this is about to happen, nor will permission be asked; it is done without the visitor to the web site even being aware of it. In other words, a piece of code which could contain a virus is written directly to a computer in a way that bypasses all virus-protection procedures. Even worse, that code itself could be malicious, designed to attack the system directly. So far four different types of attack have been identified.

System modification: Important files are altered.
Invasion of privacy: Private files can be read.
Denial of service: Preventing a computer being used for legitimate purposes.
Antagonism: More annoying than dangerous, this could, for example, constantly play an irritating piece of music until the computer is rebooted.

To be fair to Java this language has been designed to work in what has been termed a 'sandbox', which means there are barriers between it and the rest of the computer. Unfortunately, on more than one occasion loopholes have been found, through which hackers have been able to penetrate system security. Microsoft, on the other hand, has no such sandbox in its ActiveX technology, and in fact this is designed to integrate with the operating system, so that any command available to the user is potentially available to a hacker – including file deletion and disk formatting. Not only that, but in a highly controversial move Microsoft has also released plans to make Java just as integrated into the next release of its Windows operating system, which effectively eliminates that sandbox protection.

Faced with a threat like that there is only one sensible course of action for any security conscious manager to take: **Switch off the active content**. This can be done through the Windows VIEW/OPTIONS/SECURITY menu, where the option 'Allow downloading of active content' should be deselected.

So far the only commercial purpose of active content, apart from making web sites look attractive, is on the home shopping pages, which most companies could probably live without. Apart from that it has very little function in making a web site more informative, so there is very little reason to take the risks associated with active content. Leave it alone and, for good measure, regularly check the web sites of the two main suppliers of web software – both for news of the latest security breaches and to download the software needed to fix them. These are:

Microsoft: WWW.Microsoft.Com/Security
Netscape: WWW.Netscapeworld.Com

10　PC Security

Not every computer will be part of a gigantic corporate network, complete with Internet connection and sophisticated access-control routines. Some, perhaps most, will be simple PCs connected to nothing more than the office printer. Yet even these can hold precious data that must be kept away from prying eyes or protected from accidental damage. With the stand-alone PC both are equally likely. Data could be stolen by thieves or just lost by inexperienced users, with the added complication that the computer itself could be damaged or stolen.

Hardware Theft Prevention

If physical theft is likely to be a problem, for example in buildings open to the public, a quick solution is to use some form of bolt or clamp, many of which are commercially available. These might stop opportunist crime, although they would be no match for a determined thief armed with a pair of bolt-cutters. A better defence against that is to use removable hard disks. If they can be locked away safely at night, then the computer becomes useless, which should deter most thieves – assuming the fact is well advertised. Even so, those hard disks are still a weak link. (Should one go missing, it is virtually certain a computer will disappear soon after – so be warned.)

141

Even in less public environments theft is still a very real possibility. In such situations any bolts or clamps must do more than secure the base of the computer, because the plastic casing could be smashed away, giving the thief a computer for the price of a new case (which can be bought easily).

It is also possible that the thieves may not be after the PC itself but only the extremely valuable silicon chips that are its heart. There are a number of devices on the market which indelibly print a unique identifying number on the microchip. As a method of recovering stolen property this is obviously a great deal of help to the police, but (and this particular 'but' is important) the casing has to be removed in order to mark the chips, and that could invalidate the manufacturer's warranty. Before using any such device check with the manufacturer – and insist on having a reply in writing. British Telecom is reportedly having this problem, so what chance do smaller companies have?

Finally, if equipment is stolen always uprate the security system. Thieves know that equipment will be replaced by the insurance companies, and unless you improve your security they will also know that brand-new equipment is protected by security measures which they are capable of penetrating. These two factors together form an irresistible combination. Where theft is concerned, lightning very often strikes in the same place twice.

With laptops, of course, the situation is different. They are portable by design, and so are easily stolen. This means that special precautions are needed. The following actions are recommended by the Association of British Insurers:

Have a management inventory system which requires individuals to sign for a specific laptop, whether for use inside or outside the office.

Make sure that equipment is not swapped or lent to other staff without proper authorization.

142

Ensure that arrangements are made to retrieve the laptop when an individual leaves the firm.

Ensure that staff are aware of the value of equipment and the potential threat of theft.

Make staff aware that theft, either external or internal, will be reported to the police.

Consider making loss by gross negligence a disciplinary offence.

Clearly label or mark equipment.

Lock equipment in secure cupboards, even during office hours, when it is left unattended.

Secure meeting rooms when equipment is left unattended.

Encourage staff to challenge unfamiliar visitors.

Disguise carrying cases used to transport laptops (a highly visible logo increases the risk of theft or street crime).

When travelling by car always lock equipment in the boot.

Following these guidelines will not prevent theft altogether, but at the very least the insurance claim will be easier to process.

Preventing Accidental Damage

As for damage, a good percentage of that can be avoided by one simple trick. The power cable that plugs into the back of the computer usually has two screws to hold the plug in place. Leave them undone. A connection will still be made, and the computer will work, but when the inevitable happens and someone trips over the power lead the cable will simply slip out of its socket, instead of bringing the computer crashing to the floor. Any work that has not been saved will be lost, of course, but that will always be cheaper than a broken computer.

Otherwise, preventing the damage of data loss comes down to a series of Dos and Don'ts.

Never Format a Cold Disk

If a hard disk is formatted when cold, then, as it warms up and expands, the tracks will be slightly out of alignment. This can result in preventable data loss, so let the computer acclimatize to room temperature before formatting it.

Do Not Block the Air Vents

Ideally there should be at least a six-inch clearance around all the PC's air vents. This is so that the cooling fan can suck in enough air to dissipate the heat produced by its electronic components. If the temperature inside the casing does rise, the solder on the printed circuit boards could dry out and crack. The same applies to the monitor, which should never have books or drawings stacked on top of it.

Keep Expansion Slots Closed

All PCs have extra expansion slots – places where further disk drives and other add-on equipment can be fitted. These slots should always be kept closed. The machine is designed to operate this way, so leaving them open affects the air flow inside the machine and can lead to overheating.

Avoid Dust and Smoke

With its fan constantly sucking in air and its electronics producing an electrostatic field, the Personal Computer is one of the most efficient dust-collectors ever invented. This is highly unfortunate, because dust can drastically reduce its working life. A layer of dust on a circuit board can act as a thermal insulator, preventing the components underneath from being adequately cooled. Worse still, particles within the dust could conduct electricity and short-circuit the entire system. Similarly cigarette smoke can be sucked into the machine where it collects as a brown tar.

According to the companies which specialize in PC maintenance and repair, nine out of ten problems that require a service engineer are caused by dust and dirt.

Check and Maintain

If a computer is well maintained, it is less likely to break down at the critical moment. The first step towards a sound working practice has nothing to do with maintenance, yet it will do more to keep the machine in good order than anything else.

Always Shut the Computer down Properly

Windows stores temporary files on the hard disk and then deletes them at the end of each session – provided it has the chance. If the computer is switched off with Windows still running those files will be left, taking up disk space and, even worse, potentially causing the computer to crash. As these files tell Windows that files are open – and, therefore, what has to be closed – the risk of data corruption and system failure is just too great to ignore. For this reason, always exit Windows, or use the shut down procedure in Windows 95. From time to time it is also a good idea to check the directory where those temporary files are stored (usually either DOS\TEMP or WINDOWS\TEMP). Any file with the extension .TMP can be deleted – though only with Windows shut down, or else a file needed for that current session could be deleted with disastrous consequences.

After that, there are other measures that should be taken every week.

Check available Disk Space

If the hard drive becomes too full there will be no space left for Windows' temporary files and swap files, or even for new information, which will cause data to be lost. To prevent that happening, any time the hard disk becomes anywhere near ninety per cent full either delete or archive files. Give Windows enough space to work in.

Scan for Corrupted Files

Using SCANDISK, which is already available to both DOS and Windows users, the hard drive should be checked for lost files and bad sectors. (A lost file is data stored on the disk with no obvious link to any application; a bad sector is an area of the disk where the magnetic material has degraded to the point of being unusable.) SCANDISK finds lost files and marks bad sectors to prevent them being used. Additionally, if errors are found on a regular basis, this can be taken as a valuable warning of an impending disk failure.

Then, just to complete the job, every month:

Defragment the Hard Drive.

Data is written to the hard drive along magnetic tracks. When some files are deleted, this leaves blank spaces between the remaining files, which the computer attempts to fill when new work is saved to disk. Over time, this means many files can become fragmented – i.e. stored in chunks that are distributed in various different places across the disk. As a result, when working on these files the read/write head has to visit each of these places in turn, which not only means that it takes longer to read a file, it also increases wear and tear on the drive mechanism. To prevent this, software is available (and is built into Windows 95) which defragments those files by placing them into a long strip, referred to as contiguous clusters. However, as this deals with the organization of the hard disk at its most basic level it should only be done after a full backup is taken.

Do Not Over-use the Power Switch

Switching on a computer stresses its components more than anything else. As this can shorten their working life, it is best to switch the machine on in the morning and leave it on all day. However, if a badly behaving program means the computer has to be switched off to reset it, always wait before switching it back on. The microchip holds its charge for a few seconds, so before switching the power on again, give it enough time to drain to earth. Otherwise the residual charge, plus the mains power coming through, could cause it to burn out.

Set Important Files to Read-only

An inexperienced operator can do untold damage by accidentally deleting or altering important files. To prevent this use the DOS command ATTRIB to set them to Read Only. In that way, while they can still be used, no one can change or delete them. At the very least the files COMMAND.COM, CONFIG.SYS and AUTOEXEC.BAT should be treated this way.

Note all CMOS RAM Settings

All PCs have a piece of hardware called CMOS RAM (otherwise known as the BIOS, or Basic Input/Output System) which holds important information like the settings for the hard and floppy disk controllers. Without this information the computer will not even recognize its own hard disk. This is, in fact, a common problem, and the reason for it is that the settings in the CMOS RAM have been corrupted (which can happen for any number of reasons). Until those settings are restored the computer is useless.

To find out what those settings are power up the computer then immediately press the DEL key. (Depending on the manufacturer, a different key, or combination of keys, might be needed;

if so, a message will appear on screen.) This will give access to a whole range of information, all of which should be written down, but none of which should be altered. If a fault later develops this can be referred to, either so that the settings can be restored or to help the technician if further repair is needed.

For those using DOS 6.0 or Windows an easier, and safer, method is to use the Microsoft Diagnostic utility MSD. From DOS or FILE/RUN in Program Manager enter C:\WINDOWS\ MSD.EXE. Then select DISK DRIVES from the options available. To make things even easier the FILE menu at the top of the screen includes the facility to print out a report. Nothing could be simpler. Windows 95 users will, first of all, have to copy this from the Windows 95 CD-ROM as it is not included in the standard installation. It can be found in the OTHER\MSD Directory.

Preventing Data Theft and Sabotage

While protection from accidental damage can be achieved relatively easily, data theft and sabotage are unfortunately a lot harder to guard against.

DOS

The basic reason for this is that the DOS operating system was never designed to be secure. When it was first created no one expected PCs to be used outside a scientific laboratory, far less hold confidential information, so, where security should have been built in, DOS provides unlimited access to both programs and data. This means that security has to be achieved despite DOS.

That is not quite fair, because there is at least one quick fix available by which one can frustrate the curious: disabling the DIR command. This command provides a listing of all directories, and the files in those directories – something needed by anyone who wants to search the hard disk. If you want to stop that happening, you should add the line 'SET DIRCMD = O' to the AUTOEXEC.BAT file. Then, when anyone tries to use the command, all they will get is a message saying no files were found. Programs can still run, and data can still be copied, but only by those who know the file names.

As for the rest of DOS, commands such as XCOPY, FORMAT and PRINT are programs in their own right, and so a measure of security can be gained by deleting them from the hard disk. Unfortunately, it is difficult to go beyond that, because of the way DOS was designed.

There are a great many access-control (password-protection) packages on the market, but they invariably work from a batch file – which is to say they use the programming language built into DOS to create files ending in .BAT. Convenient as this may be it also suffers from the problem that any batch file can be terminated by pressing the CTRL and C keys together. By doing this, a thief can prevent the control software loading and access the system without need of a password.

One way to avoid this is to use the DOS command CTTY, which determines what input device the computer takes its commands from. Normally this would be the keyboard, but adding the line 'CTTY NUL' to the beginning of the AUTOEXEC.BAT file changes all that. Once the command has been executed the computer will only accept instructions from the NUL device, which (since there is no such thing as a NUL device) means the keyboard is effectively disabled. Then, once the protection software batch file has been run, adding the line 'CTTY CON' returns the computer to its normal operation.

Unfortunately, normal operation for DOS still means problems for the access-control software. Before looking for the system files (which install the operating system) on the hard disk, DOS first of all looks to the A: drive, the floppy disk drive. This is primarily a safety feature, so that the computer can still be made operational in the event of a hard disk problem, but from a security point of view it has serious implications. It enables anyone to by-pass all the security arrangements stored on the hard disk by starting the computer with a floppy; all it takes is a standard disk formatted with the system files.

Depending entirely on the access-control software being used, this can be counteracted in two different ways. The first, and best, is to build routines into the software which prevent this. The second – which should be avoided, as it can be defeated easily – involves the CMOS RAM (BIOS) settings. These can be accessed, as explained earlier, and when that is done one of the options available is to disable the A: drive during the boot (startup) process. This apparently solves the problem – except a thief can change it back just as easily.

Sometimes the CMOS RAM will have its own password-protection routines built in as one of the options available; if so, treat this as a luxury. The option can be used to inhibit casual thieves and keep them from using the A: drive as a point of entry into an otherwise secure system, but it should never be used for more. When the power to the computer is turned off the settings are retained in its memory by means of a small battery. All a determined thief has to do, therefore, is open the case and disconnect that battery; a few seconds later it can be reconnected and the computer powered up, having lost its protective settings.

DOS is not a secure operating system. Yet, insecure as it is, users still need to have at least a basic level of knowledge about it before they can cause any damage. For the inexperienced, the untrained or the just plain curious the real danger lies in Windows.

Windows

In many ways the versatility of Windows is its biggest drawback. Users are able to configure so much of the system to their own personal tastes that problems inevitably arise when the wrong change is made, either accidentally or maliciously. As an example of what can be done, it is even possible to have black characters printed against a black background – just ask any service engineer called out to repair a suspected faulty monitor (or ask any manager who has had to foot the bill for the call-out).

For this and other reasons many companies like to present their users with a much restricted set of options. The features most likely to cause problems can be removed, so that, while productivity is in no way affected, the potential for damage is greatly reduced. It does require alterations to the initialization (.INI) files, but this can be done using Windows' Notepad program and is simple in the extreme.

To begin with Program Manager: this uses a file called PROG-MAN.INI, to which an extra section named [RESTRICTIONS] should be added. Under this heading, include any or all of the following:

NoRun = 1: This removes the RUN command from the FILE menu, preventing users from running unauthorized software.

NoClose = 1: This removes the EXIT WINDOWS command, preventing users from leaving Windows either to run software under DOS or to use any of its commands.

NoSaveSettings = 1: This removes the SAVE SETTINGS ON EXIT command. If users alter the desktop configuration, restarting the computer brings it back to the way it was.

NoFileMenu = 1: This removes the FILE menu entirely. Users cannot create, edit or delete any application.

EditLevel = x: Here x can be a number between 0 and 4 to determine what level of security is invoked:
0: No restrictions whatsoever.

151

1: Disables the NEW, MOVE, COPY and DELETE commands in the FILE menu although users can still move icons within groups or add new items.

2: This prevents users adding, moving, copying, deleting or removing icons or changing group properties. Icon command lines can still be changed.

3: This includes all the restrictions of level 2 with the addition that users can only change icons and group properties, not command lines and group file names.

4: The highest level of security available. Users cannot even change the properties of groups or icons.

Once the new PROGMAN.INI file has been saved, restarting Windows will bring the restrictions into force.

For further protection it might be useful to prevent one or more of the Program Manager groups from being changed. Again this can be done easily. Each group has a file ending in .GRP associated with it, so changing this to Read Only (using the DOS command ATTRIB) is all it takes. The file cannot be written to, so it cannot be changed, and therefore the group cannot be changed.

While on the subject of Program Manager groups, any application can be made to run automatically by dragging its icon into the STARTUP group. This means that when the computer is first switched on users are taken directly to whatever accounts or database package they normally use. As a means of cutting down the opportunities for tinkering this is obviously first-class, but it does have the disadvantage that the application must be in the STARTUP group. For those situations where it would be preferable to keep applications and files in a separate group, yet still have them load automatically, that, too, can be catered for. In the

PROGMAN.INI file look for a section called [SETTINGS] then add the line 'STARTUP = <name>', where <name> is the group to be used. After that, saving the file and restarting Windows is all it takes.

For anyone still worried about users running DOS programs – which is a valid concern, as these days most of them are games – another trick can be used. This is based on the fact that, when DOS is run from within Windows, it must have its own Program Information File (.PIF). If a particular piece of software has no .PIF file, then Windows automatically uses DEFAULT.PIF, which is where the trick comes in. Using the PIF editor, in the MAIN group, call up this file and set both the memory required and the memory desired to zero, doing the same for EMS memory and XMS memory. These settings determine how much memory is allocated to each application, and, as that is now zero, anyone trying to run unauthorized software will get no further than a message saying 'Insufficient memory to Run Application'. Naturally any authorized software will need its own .PIF file, and the PIF editor should be deleted, but that apart the system is fool-proof.

Unfortunately with Windows there is more to worry about than DOS programs. Another problem area is CONTROL PANEL, the group which controls the screen colours and fonts, but which also controls printer and network settings. It makes good sense to remove some of the more troublesome aspects of this, which can be done very easily by adding a section to the CONTROL.INI file called [DON'T LOAD]. Under this heading write the caption for any icon not wanted, followed by '= TRUE'. For example, to stop users changing the colour, show the line 'COLOR = TRUE' (remember to spell it the American way).

Although any icon can be prevented from loading, the three most important are the network section, the printer section and 386 ENHANCED. As this controls the way Windows allocates system resources, saving this from alteration is a very good idea.

Even so, there is still a massive problem at the heart of Windows: File Manager. With this, files can be copied, moved or deleted, programs can be run and entire directories removed. In other words, no matter what has been done to make the system secure, the presence of File Manager makes it all a complete waste of time. And, just to make it worse, no restrictions can be applied. Faced with that there can be only one solution: delete File Manager.

In fact a great deal of Windows can be deleted without causing undue harm. An obvious candidate is the DOS icon, especially if other steps have been taken to keep users away from DOS. In much the same way Notepad should go, to prevent users re-editing the .INI files. Another program called SYSEDIT.EXE should also be deleted, for the simple reason that it is an alternative way of editing the major configuration files. As with the DOS commands, it is probably better to delete too much, and then reinstall it if the occasion demands, rather than leave possibly harmful files still on the disk.

For anyone who has made the switch to Windows 95 the news is mixed. While it is possible to do exactly the same as under Windows 3.1 (using the System Policy Editor on the Windows 95 CD) exactly how it should be done is something not even Microsoft admits to knowing anything about. This is what is known as an undocumented function – which means it exists on no technical specification and is therefore beyond the reach of anyone manning the telephone help lines. To make matters worse, it also involves making changes to the registry, which is such an important file – and so easily damaged – that the best advice is to keep well away.

Microsoft has promised to rectify this situation in the future, as part of its ZAW (Zero Administration for Windows) initiative. That being the case, anyone who is not an expert and does not have access to specialized Internet forums or articles in the technical journals (not to mention a death wish) can only wait. Those who are expert will probably know what to do already, but if anybody claims such expertise *insist* they back up the registry before they start.

Another very good idea for Windows 95 users is to look on the CD for a folder called ERU which can be found under OTHER\MISC. Copy this into the 'My Computer' folder and then double-click on the icon marked ERU. A message will appear on screen asking for a directory or drive to be specified, but the default offered is more than adequate. After that, a full backup copy of all the important files will be stored in a folder called ERD, together with a small piece of software that can automatically write them back to their original folders. Then, if problems are encountered, simply restart the computer and press F8 as soon as the message 'Starting Windows 95' appears. At that point yet another menu will become available, and option 5 (Command mode only) should be chosen. This prevents Windows loading and runs the computer in DOS only, at which point entering the command C:\ERD\ERD.EXE will cause that particular piece of code to run and restore all the system files back to their original settings. Thereafter simply restarting the computer is all it takes to implement these settings.

It should also be remembered that the increasing number of PCs bought for home use means that the population as a whole is becoming steadily more computer literate. What was once a mysterious box is now standard technology, with its tricks known to many. That might have its advantages, but, like all forms of progress, it also has its dangers.

11 Network Security

Of all computer systems, networks are the least secure; they combine the low security of the PC with the massive data capacities of a mainframe. Unless tightly controlled, a network could be to data what a colander is to water – a barely noticed obstruction before it disappears forever – and the threat posed by a virus to a single PC is multiplied by the number of machines connected to it. At times networking products should carry a Government Health Warning.

As proof, consider the case of Safeway supermarket employee Simon Birch. According to reports, he claimed that, due to lack of safeguards, anyone with an access password (of which there were about 20) could cause absolute chaos – to the point of being able to transfer money anywhere. How much of this is true only he and Safeway can know. There must be some truth in it, though, because the case only came to light when he was prosecuted under the 1990 Computer Misuse Act for tampering with the Barcode system. Apparently he made it appear as if £22,000 worth of groceries had vanished. This does at least highlight the kind of damage that employees can cause.

General Precautions

Nonetheless, it is possible to make networks safe, both from the malicious and the curious. The malicious are obviously those who would steal or damage corporate data. The curious can be defined as those who try a previously unused option 'just to see what happens'. These are the people who, according to one survey, waste 5.1 hours a week playing around with system settings, not realizing they could inadvertently bring the entire network crashing down (and all of it done on software supposedly designed to boost productivity). What can be done to protect users from themselves?

Consider Diskless Workstations

If a computer has no floppy disk drive, then it becomes impossible both for sensitive information to be copied and taken out of the building and also for anyone to use unauthorized software. As a consequence, the risk of virus infection is also reduced.

Store Data on Network Drives

If all data is stored on one centralized hard disk, then responsibility for its regular backup can safely be left to the Network Administrator. The alternative is to store data on local drives and hope individual users remember to take backups. The latter is never a good idea; those who believe their staff do this as a matter of routine are advised to carry out a snap inspection – and be prepared for a shock.

Restrict Free Disk Space

Where removing floppy drives is impractical, another option is to restrict the amount of disk space available to individual users.

Calculate the amount of disk space needed for the operating system and software (not forgetting the Windows swap file), add a bit extra to cater for possible upgrades, and then create a partition on the local hard disk of that size. In DOS the command to use is FDISK, which tells the computer to treat the hard drive as two (or more) entirely separate disks. These then have to be formatted (or not, if nobody is to use them), but thereafter each user will have a C: drive with no space left over. That means no space to store a game, and no space to copy sensitive data to before transferring it to a floppy when no one else is looking. For networks already operating, software now exists to repartition disk drives without disturbing the data stored on them.

Remove Default Passwords

Some systems have passwords preinstalled by the manufacturer (default passwords). These will usually be something like 'FIRST-PASS' or 'PASS1' and are there only to make setting up the system easier. Once this has been done, they should be removed. Their presence represents a potentially massive security breach, even in systems where more sensible passwords have been assigned, and for that reason alone they have to go. Having spare passwords freely available to anyone is never a good idea.

Be Careful of Fax Modems

If these are installed on a network, always set access rights to users' directories, so that faxes can only be read by the people who should read them.

Separate Hardware-specific Files from User-specific Files

Hardware-specific files should be stored on the local hard disk, while any user-specific files like special drive mappings or customized options should be stored in the home directory of the network server. The hardware-specific files should be made Read-only (using ATTRIB). This carries with it many advantages:

What users cannot touch they cannot change; what they cannot change cannot bring the system down.

In the event of a PC failure, a new machine can be plugged in and set up immediately.

If users have to work in a different part of the building for any reason, their usual system setup can easily be transferred.

Isolate Key Equipment

On a less technical note, security can be increased just by taking care over the positioning of the network server. For true security it should be behind locked doors, but where this is impossible it should at the very least be isolated from other office equipment. Then no one has an opportunity to go near it, which restricts their opportunities to tamper with the settings, introduce password monitoring programs, infect it with a virus or just switch it off (all of which comes under the heading of typical behaviour).

Consider, too, the way the printer is used. If the same printer handles both confidential and non-confidential material, then anyone collecting their own work stands a very good chance of seeing whatever else has been printed out, no matter what its security classification. The risk is the same as that of leaving a classified document in the photocopier, the only difference being that it happens on a regular basis. The only viable solution is to have two printers, one of which is kept strictly for classified information. Any other system, like not letting the staff collect their own work, or standing guard while confidential material is being printed, usually falls apart under the pressure of a busy office routine. The only truly safe method is to have a second printer and keep it out of sight.

To take network security beyond this, the problem needs to be split into the four areas of concern:

160

The workstation.
The server.
The cable.
The system.

The Workstation

This is nothing more than a stand-alone PC with an extra cable attached, so all the issues relating to PC security apply here – multiplied by the number of machines on the network. Because of the sheer volume of data that can be stored on a network, and because password security can be so easily disabled, good security means fitting a lock to the PC casing.

Some workstations come with locks fitted as standard, although others have electrical locks (which are not the same thing at all). Electrical locks just prevent the keyboard being used. Only a physical lock can protect the battery. This adds extra security without inconveniencing the user.

The Server

For servers, the issue is power in both its senses. Electrical power and the power that comes from control. The threat of someone switching off the electrical power, either accidentally or pseudo-accidentally, can be countered by a power-switch lock. Switching off the electricity supply will not do too much damage, although it could result in files being corrupted and the system being shut down for several hours. This makes a power-switch lock a sound investment, if only for the sake of productivity – especially when it is used in conjunction with an Uninterruptible Power Supply. To increase protection still further some systems offer the facility for monitoring the UPS, so that, if it switches in, an urgent message is sent across the network to the administrator. The UPS can then keep the system operational until the administrator finds the plug that has just been pulled out of its socket.

The next point might be obvious, but is still worth repeating. Any number of administrative or maintenance tasks can be carried out, from the server, and many of these give direct control over the system's resources. It therefore makes good sense to restrict all access to the server. Even if it is out of sight – which it should be – at the very least the administrator functions should be password protected.

The Cable

Yet another inherent weakness of networks is the cable running between each computer. This can be tapped into, so that data-logging devices or even complete workstations can be added without the authorization or knowledge of the administrator. For high-security environments the safest option is to use fibre optics, while for other, more mainstream situations simple inspection and testing should be enough – assuming the tests are carried out regularly.

Another method involves a TDR, or Time Domain Reflectometer. This device, available from most network special-ists, detects breaks by sending a signal down the wire and measuring the time it takes for it to return. Although at the hi-tech end of the scale, a TDR can be an invaluable tool for protecting larger networks or high-security installations.

The System

On the principle of leaving the worst until last, the system itself now has to be looked at. Here the biggest threat specific to networks is the fact that every single packet of data is sent through every single workstation on the system. That means anyone with the right equipment can monitor all the information being passed across the network. And, just to make matters worse, such equipment is easily available in the form of a LAN Analyser, which is a diagnostic tool used by support staff to locate problems on the network.

LAN Analysers are either hardware- or software-based, but the precautions against their misuse are broadly similar:

Keep them under lock and key.
Allow no sensitive work to be done while they are in use.
Once a LAN Analyser has been used, change all supervisor passwords.
Regularly check workstations for unauthorized copies of LAN Analysers installed on local hard drives.

As an added security feature, some systems offer the facility to encrypt all messages before sending them across the network, but these should be treated with extreme caution. Firstly, encrypted passwords are exactly what the dedicated thief needs, because they can be fed back into the system without arousing any suspicion. Secondly the encryption is not total; unless the printer has been modified to accept encrypted files any work to be printed will have to be sent to it in plain text, which leaves a glaring hole in the security shield. This is all the more true if a printer is dedicated to confidential material, because that gives a thief a specific target.

A hardware alternative to encryption is to use what is known as an intelligent hub. A normal hub is just a device to distribute the wiring from a single point out to a number of workstations, but an intelligent hub does much more: it checks the destination address of each data packet and sends it to that destination only – all the other workstations receive empty packets which give the thief nothing to examine. Intelligent hubs can also detect data coming from unauthorized workstations, disconnect the suspect PC and send an E-mail message to the network administrator. The suspect data is then destroyed before it can enter the system.

Access Restrictions

Of course, the real threat to a network comes from bored, curious or disgruntled employees – the people whose misuse of computer systems, according to the 1996 Information Security Breaches Survey, accounted for eighteen percent of all security breaches. Every one of these was described as serious. Obviously not all of these breaches will have been committed over a network, but there is a high chance that a significant proportion of them were. Unlike PCs and mainframes networks can at times be too fragile and far too vulnerable to system changes for their own good.

This shows clearly that even elementary precautions could pay huge dividends. On the whole, these centre around the fact that each user has an account file which specifies their rights for every drive and directory in the system, together with other security information. These can be used to restrict access in a variety of ways.

Log-in Restrictions

These cover both when and where each user can log into the network. As every workstation has its own unique identifying number, unauthorized access can be blocked simply by restricting users to individual computers. This means that no one can stay out of sight – in a private office, for example – while they tamper with the network; if they are not using their designated terminal, the system will refuse them entry.

For added security it is also possible to specify the times when a log-in request will be granted. This effectively stops casual or late-night hackers, because the system can only be used during predetermined hours.

Directory Rights

All employees should be stopped from using any directory unless they have specific permission to do so. If a user creates a subdirectory, direct permission should be granted before this can be accessed.

File Rights

Important files should be assigned special rights that prevent users from editing, deleting or copying them. This assignment should only be done by the network administrator, because some applications can crash the system if the wrong file has the wrong attributes.

Some network systems also offer a guest ID to give limited access. Needless to say this should be cancelled unless and until it is needed – and then repealed immediately afterwards.

Closed User Groups

At this point it is perhaps worth mentioning the need-to-know principle, around which all security is based. A European Commission survey (published in a book entitled *LAN Security: The Business Threat from Within*, 1991), on network security identified the increasing interconnection of systems as the biggest threat, closely followed by the spread of systems into areas without traditional accounting safeguards.

The problem is that, while each department might have its

own network, there are times when they need to communicate with each other. For example, Accounts might need the payroll information held in Personnel. The fact that they can do so, that different networks can be connected, is what makes the system at once powerful and flexible, and yet also vulnerable. If the various networks are connected, then what is to prevent someone in, say, Stock Control from searching the personnel records, or stealing marketing information?

The answer is Closed User Groups (CUG): a system designed to prevent users electronically 'walking' round the entire system. Based on the bridge – a device used to connect different networks – they will only allow users to gain entry into a particular network if they belong to the same CUG. For example, as Personnel and Stock Control will be in different groups the information held in one department is safe from the prying eyes of users in the other. All it takes is an intelligent bridge and a small amount of planning, and the biggest threat to network security is taken care of without in any way interfering with productivity.

Windows for Workgroups

Unfortunately there are still other problems to be solved, many of which can be found in Windows for Workgroups.

This network version of Windows, has the same weaknesses as the original: because it is easy to alter, users do exactly that. Fortunately, as with the stand-alone Windows, there are ways of preventing them from doing anything that could wreck the system.

Start with the share names and paths. Once these have been established, edit the WINFILE.INI file to include the line 'NoShareCommands = 1' in the [RESTRICTIONS] section. This disables the SHARE AS and STOP SHARING options on the disk menu and on the toolbar, which stops users creating new shared directories or removing those that already exist. Similarly, adding the same line to the [SPOOLER] section of the WIN.INI file prevents the share options in Print Manager being changed.

For good measure it might also be wise not to load the Network icon in Control Panel, as previously explained. Also, if a machine is dedicated to running one particular application, this can be loaded automatically from the [BOOT] section of SYSTEM.INI. There the line 'SHELL = PROGMAN.EXE' should be changed so that PROGMAN.EXE is replaced by the name of the program to be run.

After that, life starts to get complicated. Because of the poor security facilities in early versions of Windows for Workgroups, Microsoft added a utility called Admin Configurator – and then forgot to tell anyone about it. Depending entirely on the installation, it might be already loaded to a network drive, or it might still be on one of the master disks. In the latter case, look for a file called ADMINCFG.EX_ and then enter the command:

EXPAND A:\ADMNCFG.EX_ C:\WINDOWS\ADMINCFG.EXE
(EXPAND.EXE is likely to be found on disk 1)

Once decompressed, ADMNCFG.EXE has its own icon and can be set up from within Windows. Admin Configurator can then be used to:

Choose a Settings File

System settings are held in an encrypted file called WFWSYS.CFG which, if need be, could be set up on a network drive, keeping hardware- and software-specific files separate. As an added security measure, each file is coded to work only with the copy of Windows on which it was installed, so that no one can use a copy from another PC. Admin Configurator also password-protects new files automatically. To apply a password to an existing file, use the ADMIN button and then SET PASSWORD.

Limit File-sharing Facilities

File sharing can be disabled if this represents a threat to security. A user would still be able to share files on other machines; only those on his or her own computer would be off limits.

Cache Passwords

Every time a valid password is entered, it is stored in an encrypted file. Then, whenever that service is needed again, Windows automatically retries that same password. If it works the user will be allowed access; if not, a new, valid, password is asked for. This saves users from trying to remember too many passwords, but, because it means the entire system is accessible from the single password used at log-in, the risks are obvious. For sensitive data this facility should be disabled by checking the appropriate option in the Password Settings screen.

Change the Log-in Screen

The standard message which appears at the top of the Log-in screen is 'Welcome to Windows for Workgroups', which, legally speaking, could be construed as an invitation to hackers. To change this check the CUSTOM LOGON BANNER option in the Administrator Settings screen and then add a new message, preferably along the lines that unauthorized access is prohibited.

Set Up the Audit Log

Just to add the final touches to Windows security, the auditing facility should be used. This is called the Event Log and can be run by choosing the Network icon in Control Panel. The audit information then goes into a file called AUDIT.LOG which can be viewed using the NET WATCHER utility in the Network Program Manager Group

Staff Training

As ever, of course, the best security device of all is good and thorough training that makes staff aware of the issues and their importance. Mistakes will still be made (expect nothing else!), but at least that is all they will be: correctable and never-to-be-repeated errors. For example, anyone who normally sends E-mail messages to a group might accidentally send a confidential message the same way (the number of office romances discovered because of this is legendary), but the chances are it will never happen again. Sheer embarrassment will see to that!

Preventing this sort of thing happening in the first place can only come through training and staff awareness. With the mass of data currently held on modern networks, that is the one security system guaranteed to pay dividends.

12   Security in Context

Good security is a delicate balancing act between inconvenience and protection. It should neither interfere with normal working routines nor allow the computer to be put at risk. In some ways, then, it brings out the best and the worst in management practices. The best because, with so much data vulnerable to attack from a disgruntled employee, it pays an organization to treat its people well; the safest companies are those with the happiest staff. On the other side of the coin, there are few sights worse than sacked or redundant staff being marched off the premises by security guards. And yet the sad fact is no responsible manager could do anything else. Letting hurt and angry employees near confidential information does no one any favours, so, once the axe falls, they have to be removed before they can do anything they might later regret.

The whole process of protecting computers and the data stored on them is governed by five factors.

Confidentiality: Information should only be disclosed to authorized individuals at authorized times and in authorized locations.

Integrity: The information must be relied upon to be complete, accurate and true.

Availability: The information must be accessible and usable whenever it is needed.

Authenticity: Information must actually be from the claimed source and divulged only to the right, authentic, individuals.

Non-repudiation: Proving that a transaction actually took place.

The extent to which any of these are implemented can only be decided on an individual basis.

When it comes to data security, the choices are endless. Some suppliers offer software-only solutions, others are hardware-related and make use of keys or swipe cards. Apart from the price, the only other point to consider is that a key or an ID card has a physical presence, which makes it immediately obvious if it is lost or stolen; with passwords no such safety-net exists. It also has to be said that hardware-based systems have no passwords to be constantly changed and constantly forgotten, although, on the minus side, they are a lot more expensive. On balance then, low-risk systems should use passwords; medium-risk systems should use hardware; and high-risk systems should use both.

Creating a Security Culture

Staff

Even so the best solution of all is to create a security culture; in other words, make staff aware that, inconvenient as the precautions might be, effective security is in their own best interests. Because of the increasing importance of data security, psychologists are now turning their attention to the problem of how to create such a culture, and a few generalized guidelines have been defined. Although by no means exhaustive they can at least point the way.

Compare attitudes with beliefs. Most people can have a belief that something is wrong coupled with the attitude that it doesn't matter (which helps to explain the illegal copying of software). To tackle this it often helps to provide a forum where those beliefs and attitudes can be articulated, probably for the very first time. This, coupled with the relevant facts and figures to support the argument, can often cause the desired change.

Reward as well as punish. In this context a reward could be something as intangible as praise from a senior manager. The point is to use the carrot as well as the stick. This holds true for every other aspect of management theory, so why should security go against tried and tested practice.

Limit the fear. A catalogue of potential disasters is likely to be counter-productive; staff will reject the entire message. Instead balance the consequences with methods of prevention so that, for example, the cost of a virus attack both in terms of lost productivity and lost data could be set against the methods of keeping the computer system virus free. This way employees will have a target to aim for – no viruses – and a reason for trying to hit that same target.

Little and often is best. An intensive session on security one Friday afternoon followed by nothing for about the next twelve months will have a very limited impact. Better by far is to keep the message simple and constantly repeat it, perhaps backing it up with a few posters. Lectures have their place, but they should not be over-used.

Regularly change the teacher. When anyone is called on to give a lecture or provide training on any subject their attitude can often change from apathy to zealotry. Therefore, regularly change the person being called on. It might even be worth giving the job to the worst offender.

Management

If these guidelines are followed, then employees can be expected to co-operate fully. However, be warned that this will only happen if security has both the backing and the commitment of all senior management. In principle that sounds easy, but in practice it is rarely so straightforward, as one highly publicized case made clear. In 1995 Rupert Pennant-Rea resigned as Deputy Governor of the Bank of England amid tabloid stories of his affair with a journalist. The exact nature of the affair should quite properly remain private; nevertheless he did arrange for the woman concerned to bypass all security checks when she visited him at the bank. Simply stated, he drove not one coach and horses through the security procedures but several, and this illustrates the dilemma sometimes faced by senior management. In this case both the Governor and the Chancellor of the Exchequer are on record as hoping he would stay. Yet the fact remains he deliberately broke the security rules. His actions might not have put any confidential information at risk, but it could be argued his crime was much worse. He damaged the security culture – and, in asking him to stay on, his superiors showed their own lack of commitment to it.

Supposing he had stayed, how could the bank then have enforced its own security policy? No staff association or union would have allowed any of its members to be disciplined for a lesser transgression. No individual would have paid more than lip-service to the procedures so blatantly ignored by their own management, and no other official would have had the authority to maintain good security.

In short, the moral of the story is this: if anyone breaks the rules, then – no matter how competent, how valued or how senior they are – they have to go. There is no other way to create an environment in which secure working practices can flourish. That might sound harsh, but it really means no more than that rules must apply equally throughout the organization – another example of how good security is linked to good management practice.

Outside Contractors

Security rules should also apply equally to outside contractors. This means that any security requirements must be written into the contract and agreed before the work begins. This should include:

What services, and what computers, are to be made available, and when.

Permissible methods of access: user IDs, passwords, etc.

A list of named individuals who will be allowed access.

Acceptance of, and compliance with, all security procedures.

Compliance with all virus-protection procedures.

The right to monitor all activity and revoke any privileges.

A full statement of liability concerning the disclosure of information.

Full involvement of any third-party subcontractors.

The right to monitor all activity should not just be the function of a named individual, or even a department. Any employee of the organization should have the right to prevent contractors from doing something which either puts the company data at risk or is against company policy. Employees should also have the right to stop any such work immediately until a competent manager can be called on to make a ruling.

Normally the contractors would also be given a copy of the data-security policy – always assuming the company actually has such a thing. A surprising number of companies do not, and yet (like a great deal of Information Technology) all it takes to create one is common sense, not computer literacy.

The Security Policy

With a written security policy a company can spell out exactly what its security procedures are and why they are necessary. Such a full statement can also give management a clear sense of direction, because it forces it to consider the subject in detail (perhaps for the first time). For this reason alone it is often worth doing – with the added bonus that it provides a platform for senior management to demonstrate its full commitment to the issue. It is, in other words, a vital part of the process. To be effective the policy should include:

A clear statement of intent signed by senior management.
A clear statement that data theft or damage is a crime against the 1990 Computer Misuse Act, and that the company will prosecute.
A full description of all backup procedures, including who is responsible.
A full description of all anti-virus procedures, stating that everyone is responsible for implementing them.
A full description of all security procedures, including Internet security where applicable.
The DOs and DON'Ts of password creation.
Where applicable, the rules of engagement for password sharing.
The mechanism for reporting security breaches, real or suspected.
The contingency plan.

As an optional extra it would do no harm to inform staff that copying software is theft, and that this data piracy leaves both them and the company open to prosecution.

A copy of the security policy should then be given to every employee, irrespective of position or function, as a sign that good security involves everyone. To emphasize this further, compliance with all aspects of the security policy must be made a part of the formal disciplinary procedures, with new employees being made aware that the terms and conditions of their employment include full acceptance of that same policy. Once that is done, both staff and management can have a clear understanding of what is expected of them and what their responsibilities are. This is a cornerstone of any data-security policy.

Risk Handling

Another cornerstone is risk handling, sometimes known as risk management. Used in parallel with a sound data-security policy, this can be described as the last brick in the wall that every organization should build around its computer. That might sound fanciful, yet it is nothing more than a very down-to-earth procedure for deciding how each risk should be handled, once all the risks have been identified and the various options considered. Briefly, there are four ways of dealing with any problem.

Avoidance

If a service, facility or method of working carries with it an unacceptable level of risk, then it should be discontinued. Doing this is not a failure to implement effective security procedures, because this is a case where the costs of security far outweigh its benefits. Care must also be taken to make sure that changing circumstances do not reintroduce the problem in a different guise.

An obvious example here would be the threat posed to Internet users by Java and ActiveX (collectively known as Active Content). As already explained in Chapter 9 they represent a serious risk yet their use has no business justification, therefore configure the corporate computer not to accept them from Internet web pages. Avoid the risk.

Retention

If the risk is slight, or the loss would have only minor consequences, while countermeasures would be expensive or difficult to maintain, then it might be decided to take no counter measures; the organization could be prepared to bear any losses that occur as the price of the benefits the service offers. This should not be confused with a failure to identify the risk. The possible frequency of the losses should also be taken into consideration, however, because a small loss occurring repeatedly could have the same financial impact as a large loss which happens only once.

Any organization taking this option must carefully monitor the situation and be prepared to take action should the losses increase to an unacceptable level.

A good example of this in practice can be seen in Chapter 9. Under the section dealing with people logging on to the company computer from outside the office it was recommended that the computer be re-booted if the telephone call was interrupted as this was often a sign of illegal activity. Unfortunately if the phone line was unreliable this could cause a major loss of productivity due to the computer constantly being re-booted. In other words a choice has to be made between the demands of security and the demands of productivity. If the risk of data loss is small while the loss of productivity is great then the computer could be set not to re-boot itself at every interruption. The risk of not terminating a call at the first sign of what could be illegal activity will be retained because – after serious consideration of the consequences – the productivity cost of implementing that security feature was greater than the potential data loss.

The argument might be valid, but it still bears repeating that anyone adopting it must continually monitor that known risk – and be prepared to change tactics if the cost proves greater than expected.

Reduction

The severity of any potential loss can be reduced by selecting appropriate countermeasures. These might result in extra costs, in which case those costs will have to be weighed against the benefits, or it might be possible to use different countermeasures to achieve the same result without any extra expenditure. For example keeping unauthorized personnel away from a secure area increases security for no cost whatsoever, although if physically locking the secure area is the only way to deny unauthorized access then the cost of those door locks is the cost of the counter measures.

Transfer

Where the costs associated with a particular risk are too much in themselves, it can sometimes be possible to transfer those costs elsewhere. The most obvious examples of this are security or maintenance contracts. In the same way, insurance policies are another method of risk transference, although here care must be taken. An insurance policy will often cover only the cost of the computer, not the infinitely more valuable data stored on it. Companies might also find that laptop computers are excluded from some policies, or else, if they are included, that the policy does not cover theft from cars.

Maintenance contracts should also be looked at carefully. Companies will frequently guarantee a response time of just a few hours, but that does not mean the computer will be repaired then. Usually a service engineer will arrive within the agreed time, only to confirm that the computer has indeed broken down.

The maintenance company will then quote a delay of two or three days before it can be fixed – assuming the parts are in stock (if not, there will be a longer delay while the parts are ordered – most probably from Taiwan).

Staff Organization

As by now should be obvious, the whole business of computer and data security consists of very little more than common sense. Some technical knowledge is needed, naturally, but not as much as most people seem to think. For example, the need-to-know principle which governs most security procedures is only common sense, as is the segregation of duties: not allowing anyone to audit their own work.

In pure security terms this segregation of duties can be achieved by appointing one person as security administrator and another as security auditor. The administrator is responsible for the creation and implementation of all security procedures, while the auditor checks that they are being followed and that they are effective. If staff want to report a security breach or area of weakness, it is the auditor they contact, not the administrator.

In practical terms this means any flaws in the system will be looked at impartially and not played down by anyone who regards a criticism of their system as a criticism of them. Unfortunately, it does mean that feathers could be ruffled from time to time – but that will always be a small price to pay for good security. For the same reason, network administrators should be allowed to concentrate on the day-to-day running of the network, without being involved in either the administration or auditing of security. That way when a senior manager is called in to arbitrate between conflicting points of view, or personalities, of the security auditor and the security administrator the network administrator will always be available to provide advice and technical know-how – both of which will be needed.

This might be a simple trick, but simple tricks often work. For another, try matching the level of security checks to the grade of the employee. If this is possible, then what could be seen as an inconvenience can instead be sold as a status symbol: a sign of the important work that particular employee does. In corporate life such things are important.

The only other point to keep in mind is that, no matter how secure the organization, never boast about it. To do that would be tantamount to challenging every hacker in the world, which is something security-conscious managers could well do without. Instead they should be spending their time maintaining that good security.

To sum up, then, good security is not difficult, nor is it necessarily expensive. Rather it should be seen as no more than a collection of related actions, each one important in itself, which together create a secure working environment. Regular data backup, a sound anti-virus policy, anti-theft measures and viable security procedures all supported by a workable contingency plan are the pieces of the jigsaw which must all fit together until the picture is complete.

There may be those who object to changes in their working practice as all of these measures are implemented, but they should be ignored. Good security is too important to be side-tracked by a few complaints from people who just dislike change, especially when they will equally benefit from the advantages. So force the changes through and if the complaints still persist always remember there is one argument which is unanswerable:

The true benefit of a secure computer is a secure job.

Glossary of Terms

Active Content The animated or active sections of an Internet web site designed to make the web site more visually stimulating.

ActiveX Software which creates active content, produced by Microsoft. (*See also* Java.)

A: Drive The disk drive which reads floppy disks.

Applet The tiny program embedded in an Internet web site which makes the active content work (pronounced App-let as it is a small application).

Application A substantial piece of software designed to do a particular job. (Spreadsheets and wordprocessing packages are frequently referred to as applications).

Archived When files are removed from a computer to be stored elsewhere they are said to be archived.

Audit Log An automatically created document showing who has accessed each individual file on the computer and when they did it.

Autoexec.Bat A small file which executes automatically when a Personal Computer is started up. Its main purpose is to load other pieces of software which customizes the computer to an individual user's requirements.

Boot Up The term used to describe the exact sequence of steps needed to start up a Personal Computer. The name comes from the idea that in the morning someone puts on their shoes (boots) and then fastens them in place with shoe laces (which in America are called boot straps).

Browser The software needed to access Internet web pages.

Business Resumption Planning Another name for Contingency Planning.

Cache A temporary data store held by the computer before the data is stored permanently to disk.

CAD Computer Aided Design.

C: Drive The name for the internal disk built into all Personal Computers.

Clean Room A room kept free from even the most microscopic traces of dust so sealed units (like disk drive mechanisms) can be opened, repaired and then re-sealed without contamination.

Cluster Sometimes called a file allocation unit this is the smallest amount of space on a disk to which a file can be allocated. Large files may take several such clusters, but any space not taken up by a file remains unused.

Cold Boot The act of physically turning on a personal computer. (*See also* boot up and warm boot.)

Config.sys A file which operates automatically when a personal computer is switched on to configure the system according to the components installed in it, e.g. the CD-ROM player. Config.Sys operates before Autoexec.Bat.

Contiguous Clusters Clusters on a disk which are physically located one after the other. If they hold sections of the same data file this makes reading from the disk easier and faster.

Data Cache *See* cache.

Default The standard settings for any piece of software, e.g. the colour scheme or directories to which work will be saved. Default settings can be changed at the discretion of the user.

Delete When a file is stored on a disk a reference to it is inserted in the file allocation table or FAT and the space the file takes up on the disk is marked as reserved. Deleting a file removes the entry to it in the FAT and allows the space it occupied to be used for storing other files, but until that space is physically over-written with new data that file still exists on the disk. (*See* un-delete.)

Directory A way of organizing storage space on a computer disk. Related files can be grouped together in a single directory, or sub-directory, making them easier to find.

Directory Rights Literally the right to access a particular directory on the computer which would only be allowed to authorized personnel.

Diskette Another term for a floppy disk. The material of the disk itself is extremely thin and therefore floppy. It is the material of its casing which is rigid.

Disk Operating System Routines built into a personal computer which control the way it operates.

Disk Sector A computer disk is divided into sectors like the pieces of a pie. As each sector is numbered the computer can then find a particular file simply by knowing which sector it is stored in.

DOS *See* Disk Operating System.

Download The process of electronically transferring a computer file from one computer to another.

FAT *See* File Allocation Table.

File Allocation Table An area on a computer disk which holds the physical location of all files stored on that disk.

Floppy Disk Small, highly portable disks to which data from a computer can be copied. These disks can then be inserted into another personal computer and the data transferred to that second computer.

Folder In Windows 95 a Directory is referred to as a Folder.

Format The process of electronically marking a computer disk so it can be divided into sectors. Formatting a disk removes all files stored on that disk.

.GRP A designator used by Windows to signify which files should be grouped together. A .GRP file is simply a list of related files.

Hard Disk A term used for the internal or C: drive on a personal computer.

Hard Drive Another term used to describe the C: Drive on a personal computer.

Hardware The circuit boards, components and microchips which together make up a computer.

Internet Service Provider A company which provides a link to the Internet. The service it provides is access to the Internet.

ISP *See* internet service provider.

Java The software used to create active content on an Internet web page (*see also* ActiveX).

LAN *See* local area network.

Local Area Network A system for connecting computers which are physically located in a small area, e.g. a single office.

Macro Small programming systems built into wordprocessing or spreadsheet applications to automate routine tasks.

Mainframe A large powerful computer which can typically service the needs of many users simultaneously.

Memory Manager The memory on a personal computer is divided into several areas. Memory managers see to it that each piece of software is installed into the right area for optimum efficiency. They are usually loaded by Config.Sys.

Mission Critical An operation or service which the organization cannot live without, e.g. controlling a manufacturing process or holding customer orders in a telephone sales operation.

Modem The device which connects computers to a telephone line for Internet access, bulletin boards or E-mail.

Net Surfing *See* web surfing.

Network Server On a network the server is the computer which holds all the data generated by anyone using the network.

Operating System A series of standard routines built into every computer which allow it to operate in a known manner so that computer programmers can use these routines in their own programs, e.g. the print command in a wordprocessor

186

calls the operating system routine which handles print functions. In personal computers the operating system is either DOS or Windows 95. In mainframes the operating system is UNIX.

Personal Computer Small computers designed to fit on a desk top for the use of a single individual. The computer is personal to that individual.

PGP *See* pretty good privacy.

Pretty Good Privacy A data encryption program made freely available and now used as the basis for some file encryption software.

Privileges On a network anyone who has the right to use a restricted directory is said to have the privilege of that directory.

Program A logical series of instructions given to a computer which it performs (executes) in strict order. This can also be known as software.

RAM Random Access Memory. The silicon-based memory of a computer. Software is loaded into RAM from where it is accessed by the computer as needed. As no one can predict what part of the software will be needed by the computer at a specific time (i.e. the demand is random) the memory must be capable of similarly random access. When the computer is switched off all data stored in RAM is lost.

Read-only A setting or attribute of a file which means it cannot be deleted or altered, but it can still be read. It is therefore read-only.

Re-boot The process of resetting a computer back to its initial state, i.e. when it was first switched on. (*See* warm boot).

Registry In Windows 95 the registry is a highly complex file where all the settings for the personal computer are stored. Unless great care is taken when modifying this the computer could become unworkable.

ROM Read-Only Memory. A piece of silicon where instructions are permanently stored. The computer cannot write new instructions to this (it is read-only), but instructions written into it during manufacture can be retained when the computer is switched off. This makes it ideal to hold the initial start-up instructions for the personal computer, telling the computer what files to load next and where to find them on the disk.

Sector *See* disk sector.

Server *See* file server.

Service Provider *See* internet service provider.

Software Although generally taken to mean computer programs software can also be data files, pictures or anything else capable of being stored on a computer disk.

Software Licence The kind of software which is a computer program is not bought from a company but licensed from them. This licence which is specific to a particular version of the program covers how many people are allowed to use copies of the software at any one time. It is illegal to use more copies of the program than that or to make extra copies of it for private use.

Sub-Directory If a directory has several other directories branching from it these are referred to as sub-directories.

Surfing the Internet *See* web surfing.

Swap File A section of the hard disk which is used by Windows to store any piece of software too big to fit into the available memory of a personal computer. When that piece of software is needed any other software currently in memory is written to the swap file and the needed software written to memory, i.e. the two are swapped.

Un-delete As a deleted file is not physically removed from the computer disk (see delete) un-delete simply rebuilds its entry in the FAT and reserves the space on disk taken up by that file. The file can then be read by the computer in the usual manner.

UNIX The operating system used by mainframe computers.

WAN *See* Wide Area Network.

Warm Boot Another term used to describe resetting or re-booting the computer. It comes from the idea that if a shoe (boot) is taken off during the day it will still be warm as opposed to being put on first thing in the morning when it will be cold (*see* cold boot).

Web Page A particular location on the World Wide Web which is read by a browser.

Web Site A collection of related web pages.

Web Surfing The process of continuously jumping from web page to web page.

Wide Area Network Computers connected together over a wide geographical area. Typically this would be something like computers in one office being connected to computers in another office which could be located in another city.

Windows 3.1 Software for personal computers which provides a graphical display of any applications or files stored on the hard disk.

Windows 95 A more complex version of Windows. Unlike Windows 3.1 this does not work alongside the operating system, but is instead an operating system in its own right.

WIN.INI A file which is run automatically whenever Windows is used. It sets up (initializes) Windows according to the software installed and the user's own preferences.

Work Station A personal computer which is part of a network i.e. connected to a network file server.

World Wide Web The collective name for all the web sites on the Internet.

Index